"I've never had a conversation with Neale Donald Walsch that didn't expand my thinking and touch my heart, and reading *The Essential Path* has the same effect. At a time when we so need hope, Neale shows us where to find it."

—Marianne Williamson

"I'm tempted to stand on street corners and hand out this crystal-clear book because it's an answer to our challenging times. Read it immediately—and you will soar with conviction. You may no longer doubt your purpose or your place. You just may make the bravest decision you've ever made."

—Tama Kieves, best-selling author of *Thriving Through Uncertainty: Moving Beyond Fear of the Unknown and Making Change Work for You*

"Neale Donald Walsch has done it again with a superb book that changes our relationship to self, the earth, and spirit. This essential volume shows us the path forward through our alienation, fear, and division. Written in Neale's simple yet deeply moving style, this book poses both important questions and shares critical answers that guide us to redefine and renew our understanding of what it means to be human, as individuals and as a collective."

—HeatherAsh Amara, author of *The Warrior Heart Practice* and *Warrior Goddess Training*

THE

ESSENTIAL

PATH

OVERCOMING FEAR AND FINDING
FREEDOM IN AN EVER-CHANGING
WORLD

NEALE DONALD WALSCH

ST. MARTIN'S
ESSENTIALS
NEW YORK

Published by St. Martin's Essentials, an imprint of
St. Martin's Publishing Group

www.stmartins.com

Designed by Steven Seighman

The Library of Congress has cataloged the hardcover edition as follows:

Names: Walsch, Neale Donald, author.
Title: The essential path : making the daring decision to be
    who you truly are / Neale Donald Walsch.
Description: First [edition]. | New York : St. Martins Essentials, 2019.
Identifiers: LCCN 2019001796| ISBN 9781250218834 (hardcover) |
    ISBN 9781250218841 (ebook)
Subjects: LCSH: Self-actualization (Psychology) | Self-acceptance.
Classification: LCC BF637.S4 W353 2019 | DDC 158.1—dc23
LC record available at https://lccn.loc.gov/2019001796

ISBN: 978-1-250-77964-9 (trade paperback)

Our books may be purchased in bulk for promotional, educational,
or business use. Please contact your local bookseller or the Macmillan
Corporate and Premium Sales Department at 1-800-221-7945, extension
5442, or by email at MacmillanSpecialMarkets@macmillan.com.

First St. Martin's Essentials Trade Paperback Edition: 2023

10 9 8 7 6 5 4 3 2 1

CONTENTS

1

THE PROPOSITION

We're one decision away from a solution to humanity's biggest problem.

This is a decision so powerful in its impact that it would solve not only our species' biggest *collective* problem, but the largest problem faced by every individual reading this right now.

But be warned. This decision may not be what it seems—and it *definitely* will not fall in line with what is most widely expected or most generally accepted.

That makes it a daring decision. Perhaps the most significant decision of your life. And don't think you didn't know that when you started reading here. You knew exactly what you were doing.

And why.

Nobody has to tell us that life on our planet is not what we had hoped it would be. All we have to do is take a look at what's happening every day around the world—and in some cases, in our own lives.

There are very few among us who have not found ourselves shaking our heads in discouraged dismay at the latest tweet or

online news bulletin or newspaper headline. And sometimes—
too many times, perhaps—at the challenges confronted in our
home.

This leads to a compelling question: Is it possible—just
possible—that there's something we don't fully understand
about ourselves, about life, and about God, the understanding
of which would change everything?

To me the answer is obvious. Is it to you?

If your answer is yes, you're invited to now undertake a very
quick but deeply revealing explanation of everything—why
things are the way they are on Earth today, when our biggest
problem arose, what has blocked us from the obvious solution,
and how we can dissolve the problem virtually overnight.

We begin with some additional compelling questions.

THE QUESTIONS

What if the most wonderful ideas you ever had about life were true?

What if the most wonderful ideas you ever had about yourself were true?

What if the most wonderful ideas you ever had about God were true?

What if the most wonderful ideas you ever had about what happens after you die were true?

What would then be true for you?

Do you think there would be any difference between how you might *then* experience life and how you *now* experience life?

Your answers to these questions are now setting the course and direction of your experience on Earth, did you know that?

Not to be overly dramatic about it, but it's true. They are determining the path you will take.

And humanity's *collective* answers to these questions are now creating the future of our species by determining the path we will *all* take.

Will it be the path that our species has taken for thousands of years—the one that got us here, where our lives and the world are today? Is this where we want to be? Is this our most wonderful idea about life? About ourselves? About God?

Ideas are important. It is ideas that create beliefs, beliefs that create behaviors, behaviors that create experience, and experience that creates reality. And if our most *wonderful* ideas become our beliefs, life on our planet will look much different than it does today.

Cognitive scientists tell us that all it takes is one in ten people to emphatically embrace an idea, and the mass will follow. What, then, could *cause* just one in ten people to believe that the most wonderful ideas we ever had are true?

A single decision.

We're one decision away.

Really.

But we must make that decision now. Not doing so is starting to have, on all of us, a very real effect.

3

THE EFFECT

Let's not dance around this. We have a big problem here. On Earth, I mean. And it's touching our lives every day. Individually and collectively.

There's no reason to move into a dark or depressed state over this, though, because the solution really *is* just one decision away. And it's not even a difficult decision to make. We just have to choose to make it.

Many people agree with the decision intuitively already. They simply haven't implemented it in their lives as a practical matter, probably because they're waiting to see if anyone else agrees. But the time for waiting is over.

The problem now confronting us is becoming pervasive. It's evidenced not only in the world's governments and the world's corporations and the world's social or religious institutions. It's affecting all of us. In individual homes all across the planet, we're feeling the effect.

So what's up? What's the problem? Let's lay it out in direct terms.

Humanity's biggest problem is that humanity doesn't know what humanity's biggest problem is.

We can see the *effect* of this problem all around us, but we don't seem to see the cause.

Now, you have a real problem when you know you *have* a problem, but don't understand what the problem is. You don't know what's causing the effect that you're observing every day. And humanity's confusion about this has gone on for so long that it's now created a *condition*. A condition that's threatening to become permanent.

Here's one way that it shows up: Perhaps more than ever in recent times, we're hearing folks say that if we *do* have a problem right now, it's only because of "those others" who are *creating* problems. We didn't have these problems before, these folks say, and we want to go back to the Good Old Days.

And just who, exactly, are those "others" to whom these folks are referring?

It's those unwanted immigrants, those unsatisfied minorities, those unhappy women, those right-wing radicals, those left-wing nut jobs, those unacceptable gays, those uninformed students, those dumb conservatives, those empty-headed liberals, those unmotivated government assistance recipients. It's those "others" who just keep making things difficult.

A well-known political strategist in the United States, Brad Todd, crystalized all of this in a tweet he posted in mid-2018: "Is the American Left willing to live with and among the American Right? Or are we at culture rupture?"

And the phenomenon is not limited to the United States, but is emerging all over the world. Newspaper columnist Paul

Krugman put it this way in an opinion piece in the *New York Times* written at about the same time: "The real crisis is an up-surge in hatred—unreasoning hatred that bears no relationship to anything the victims have done."

I resonate with the urgency of Mr. Todd's questions and I concur with Mr. Krugman's observations. Suddenly it feels as if we live in a world of *us* vs. *them*. People around the globe are lining up on one side or the other, and the middle ground seems to be disappearing.

Not everyone may feel this way, but everyone can *feel* everyone who feels this way. So it's affecting all of us. Each day it's producing distressing headlines, angry blogs, name-calling speeches, childish rants in tweets, bullying diatribes, finger-pointing tirades, and violence-laden outbursts.

And while we may not know the *underlying* cause of the problem human society is now facing, the cumulative *impact* of that problem can be put into a single word.

Alienation.

We are seeing it more and more. It is an outgrowth of a very contentious and unhappy situation.

THE SITUATION

Alienation inevitably arises in the aftermath of ongoing citizen frustration. Citizen frustration inevitably arises in the aftermath of ongoing societal dysfunction. Societal dysfunction inevitably arises in the aftermath of ongoing systemic failure. And that's exactly what we've had here. Long-term, ongoing, systemic failure.

We've put into place on our planet a wide assortment of systems created to make life better for all of us. Those systems are not working. There are some rare exceptions, but in the main, most are failing to produce the outcomes they were intended to produce.

Wait. It's worse. They're actually producing the opposite.

Our political systems—created to produce safety and security for the world's nations and their people—have in the main produced far too much of *exactly the opposite:* ongoing disagreements, endless insulting and demonizing of opponents, dangerous trade wars, nerve-racking military threats, and escalating violence between people at every level.

Our economic systems—created to produce opportunity

and sufficiency for all—have in the main produced far too much of *exactly the opposite:* massive economic inequality and increasing poverty, with a handful of people (actually fewer than ten) holding more wealth and resources than 3.5 *billion* (that's half the planet's population) combined.

Our social systems—created to advance and facilitate the joy of living in community and build a foundation for harmony among a divergent population—have in the main produced far too much of *exactly the opposite:* discordance, disparity, prejudice, and despair . . . with limited opportunity for upward mobility and in far too many cases rampant injustice producing exasperation and outrage.

(Even our vaunted online Internet systems—created as the newest innovation of our social systems and originally designed to bring us closer together through the "marvel" of social media—have in the main produced far too much of *exactly the opposite:* a playing of one against another through the manipulation of emotions, a heightening of our differences, an exacerbation of our fears, and a poisoning of our minds with negativity, all of which has *not* brought us closer together, but driven us further apart.)

And saddest of all, our spiritual systems—created to inspire a greater love of God, and so, of each other—have in the main produced far too much of *exactly the opposite:* bitter righteousness, shocking intolerance, widespread anger, deep-seated hatred, and self-justified violence.

Now you may think that I have exaggerated the impact of all this. Things are better here on Earth now than ever before, right? Well, I suppose that's true for some, but do you know that on this day over 1.7 billion people will have no access to clean water? Do you know that 1.6 billion will live without electricity? Do you know that, difficult as it may be to believe, 2.5 billion people—over a quarter of this planet's population—will not have toilets to use in this, the first quarter of the 21st century?

These are more than simple inconveniences. The heath hazards caused by such conditions lead to thousands of unnecessary deaths each year. And speaking of unnecessary deaths, consider this statistic: More than 650 children die of starvation every hour on this planet.

Every *hour*.

Starvation? *Really?* While we throw away more food in restaurants from Toyko to Paris to Los Angeles each evening than would be needed to feed the children of an entire outlying Third World village for a week?

Even a quick overview of such numbers—even the most dispassionate glance—surely provides dismaying evidence of our absolute, complete, and utter failure to grasp (much less activate) the simplest and most basic answers to the simplest and most basic questions that members of any sentient species would (one would think) sooner or later have to ask: Who *are we?* Who do we *choose to be* as a species?

What gives here? What's going on with the human race that it cannot see itself even as it looks at itself? Where is humanity's blind spot? What is the reason for all this?

THE REASON

Sooner or later every thinking person comes around again to this question: Is it possible—just *possible*—that there is something we don't fully understand about ourselves, about life, and yes, about God . . . the understanding of which would change everything?

It's time to ask that question everywhere. In the pews of our houses of worship, in the halls of our lawmaking bodies, in the boardrooms of our global corporations and the back rooms of our small businesses, in the town squares of our cities, in the dining rooms of our friends, and in the homes of our families.

I'm going to invite you to memorize that question and ask it wherever you go. Wherever good conversation and meaningful exchange and serious problem-solving is taking place, *ask the question*.

Then, as the question hangs in the air, explain *why* the answer is, obviously, *yes*.

We are a very young species. A lot of people like to think of humans as highly evolved. In fact, humanity has just emerged from its infancy on this planet. In their book *New World New Mind,* Robert Ornstein and Paul Ehrlich placed this in perspective in one mind-boggling paragraph:

"Suppose Earth's history were charted on a single year's calendar, with midnight January 1 representing the origin of the Earth and midnight December 31 the present. Then each day of Earth's 'year' would represent 12 million years of actual history. On that scale, the first form of life, a simple bacterium, would arise sometime in February. More complex life-forms, however, come much later; the first fishes appear around November 20. The dinosaurs arrive around December 10 and disappear on Christmas Day. The first of our ancestors recognizable as human would not show up until the afternoon of December 31. Homo sapiens—our species—would emerge at around 11:45 pm . . . and all that has happened in recorded history would occur in the final minute of the year."

I consider that to be a brilliant piece of writing. In just 125 words these two gentlemen have turned a huge piece of information into bite-sized data that we can get our head around, then more easily understand why we are continuing to act the way we do, and have not yet, as a global species, made the Daring Decision.

Our youth as a species doesn't justify our actions, but it helps us to see the nature of the challenge. We simply have to grow up. We have to stop acting like children. And we have to do it now. Today. Not in ten or twenty years. Now. Right now.

We have to stop the saber rattling—the "my missile is bigger than yours" flexing of military muscles between nations that could easily lead, on a moment's notice, to the deaths of hundreds of thousands and the decimation of nations.

We have to stop the disaster-ignoring—the kind of "look the other way" apathy that results in those statistics of the billions suffering even today on our planet due to problems we could easily solve.

We have to stop the hypocrisy—the kind of "say one thing and do another" behavior that allows us to deliberately kill people under the authority of the State in order to teach people that deliberately killing people is not okay; that allows us to place our children in front of video games and television programs and movies that depict violence, violence, and more violence, even as we talk of raising a generation that we hope will not think of violence as a first resort in conflict resolution, and will, in fact, actually renounce it.

We have to stop the kind of "ignore what's good for us" habits that allow us to consume unhealthy food, habitually inhale carcinogens, and irresponsibly drink harmful amounts of brain-frying and liver-damaging liquids, all the while preaching wholesome living.

We have to stop archaic thinking—the kind of "stuck in yesteryear" approach to life that keeps us trapped in an ancient story of civilization that motivates each of us to seek first to meet our individual needs, each of us to serve our individual agenda, and each of us to cater to our individual desires, even if it means doing so at the expense of others who we see as not part of "us."

We have to stop, just *stop,* behaving the way we have been, and call forth from within us a New Way to be Human—a way that allows us to embrace singularity without creating separation, to express differences without producing divisions, and to experience contrasts without generating conflicts.

All of this is possible, but it will require us to do something very brave. We will have to go against the grain, to adopt a way of life that only a handful have embraced throughout human history. We have to ask, when we confront and witness our own behaviors, "What are we choosing?" and . . . "Why are we choosing this?" Then we have to ask, "Why not choose God?" And we have to understand what we *mean* when we invite ourselves to choose God.

We have to be clear that the question we are asking is: Why not choose God to be experienced as a part of us, and as that of which all beings and all aspects of life are comprised?

The great irony is that the tiny handful who have taken this path, who have embraced this way of life, are the very humans we say we honor the most—even as we have declined to adopt their way of life ourselves. So what we honor in others we have dismissed as being irrelevant to ourselves.

Or perhaps it *is* relevant to ourselves, we say, but it is virtually impossible for us to experience. This, despite the fact that those humans who have done so *have told us exactly how we may do so also.*

Now, to be fair to humankind, we have certainly undertaken efforts to find an answer to our problems. Many efforts. The difficulty is not that we haven't *tried,* the difficulty is *how* we've tried. There is no fault to be found in our intention, the error lies in the manner in which we have made our attempts.

6

THE ATTEMPTS

For a very long time we have been taking a dead-end street in our attempts to address humanity's problems. We're continuing to do so to this very day.

To put it in a sentence, we keep trying to solve humanity's problems *at every level except the level at which the problems exist.*

This is because, as noted at the outset, we are not clear about the *cause* of the problems. So . . .

. . . we try first to solve our problems as if they were political problems, because we're used to using political pressure on this planet to get people to do what they don't seem to want to do.

We hold discussions, we write laws, we pass legislation and adopt resolutions in every local, national, regional, and global language and assembly we can think of to try to "legislate morality." We think we can solve the problem with words. But it doesn't work. Whatever short-term solutions we may create evaporate very quickly, and the problems re-emerge. They will not go away.

So we say, "Okay, these are not political problems, and they cannot be solved with political means. They must be economic problems." And because we are used to using economic power on this planet to get people to do what they don't seem to want to do, we then try to "buy morality." We think we can solve the problems with money.

We throw money at them, or withhold money *from* them (as in the form of sanctions), seeking to solve the problems with cash-flow manipulations. But it doesn't work. Whatever short-term solutions we may create evaporate very quickly, and the problems re-emerge. They will not go away.

So we say, "Okay, these are not economic problems, and they cannot be solved by economic means. They must be military problems." And because we are used to using military might on this planet to get people to do what they don't seem to want to do, we then try to "force morality." We think we can solve the problems with weapons.

We threaten (if we do not actually *decide*) to shoot missiles at them and drop bombs on them. But it doesn't work. Whatever short-term solutions we may create evaporate very quickly, and the problems re-emerge. They will not go away.

So, having run out of solutions, we declare: "These are not easy problems. No one expected that they could be fixed overnight. This is going to be a long, hard slog. Many lives may be lost in trying to solve these problems. But we are not going to give up. We are going to solve these problems if it kills us." And we don't even see the irony in our own statements.

After a while, however, even primitive beings of very little consciousness become tired of all the killing in battle, and all the suffering and dying of women and men, children and elderly, from the ravaging effects of ongoing conflict. And so, after enough of these tragic consequences have arisen with no solution in sight, we say it is time to call a truce and hold peace talks. And the cycle begins again . . .

We're back to the bargaining table, back to politicking as a solution. And peace talks often include discussion of reparations, the end of sanctions, and assistance in economic recovery. And so we're back to manipulating money as a solution. And when these solutions fail to work in the long run, we're back to threats and the actual use of weapons again.

On and on and on it goes. And on and on it *has* gone throughout human history. The names of the principal actors and the types of weapons have changed, but the script has not.

This is, of course, the classic definition of insanity: *doing the same thing over and over again, expecting to get a different result.*

Only primitive cultures and primitive beings do this. Yet we can't seem to—or simply *won't*—change our ways, because we are very used to trying to force solutions in our world. Yet solutions that are forced are never solutions at all. They are simply postponements.

The great tragedy and the great sadness of humanity is that we are forever willing to settle for postponements in place of solutions. Highly evolved beings would never, ever settle for postponement after postponement in solving their biggest problems.

It is difficult to believe that it was in 1879, in his last public address, that Victor Hugo prophesied: "In the twentieth century war will be dead . . . hatred will be dead, frontier boundaries will be dead, dogmas will be dead . . ."

The Wikipedia entry on this revered French poet, novelist, and dramatist tells us that "throughout his life Hugo kept believing in unstoppable humanistic progress." I would add here that what he clearly didn't imagine was that humans would take so long to gather the courage to face the largest problem of our species head on.

We've done an endless dance all around it, with the result that we continue, century after century, to try to solve the world's problem at every level except the level at which the problem exists.

We've been doing the same thing in our personal lives. First we try to solve our individual problems by talking and bargaining and "politicking" our way out of them. (Nobody has to tell us about "office politics." And yes, there are even politics in our own families and our own homes.)

If that doesn't work, we throw money at them, or withhold money from them—spending wildly to try to buy our way to happiness, or imposing strict household budgets to try to economize our way there.

If that doesn't work, we use force. Yelling, banging of fists on tables, slamming of doors, domineering discussions, ugly ultimatums, and then the ultimate personal power play: tearing up agreements, breaking promises, dissolving business partnerships, walking away from relationships, and ending marriages—all hopefully, but not inevitably, without physical violence.

Does it seem like it's time to take our blindfolds off and see the circumstance for what it is?

The problem facing humanity today is not a political problem, it is not an economic problem, and it is not a military problem.

The problem facing humanity today is a spiritual problem, and it can only be solved by spiritual means.

We must, as a civilization, begin to examine our most sacred beliefs.

7

THE BELIEFS

"Belief" is in many ways just a shorter word for "spirituality." It's a more friendly word, a less threatening or confronting word, but it refers to the same thing: what we hold dear, what we hold to be our most sacred truth.

Beliefs are tricky. They can support you or they can defeat you. As an individual, and as a collective.

Currently on planet Earth billions of people—let's call them Group One—believe that our existence continues after this present physical experience, as non-physical entities living eternally.

They also believe that *how* our existence continues, whether as an experience of wondrous joy or an experience of agony, depends on what we do or do not do, believe or do not believe, while on Earth.

In their view we've simply "found" ourselves here, having had nothing to do with our arrival, but having everything to do now with what happens after our departure.

These beliefs are, with minor variations, the underpinnings of most of the world's major religions.

Many other people—Group Two—do *not* believe that we exist eternally. They believe that their life is a biological incident, the result of certain and particular chemical interactions of others, and that life ends with the termination of their own chemical interactions. They believe that at the time of what is called "death," they simply cease to be.

And still others—Group Three—believe that we existed *before* this present physical life and that we will, indeed, exist *after* this life, with our self-consciousness and self-awareness and our sense of a particular identity very much intact.

They also believe that we are each aspects of the Essential Essence of the Universe (which some people call Divinity), that this is our True Nature, and that, therefore, the quality or environment of our eternal existence has nothing to do with reward or punishment.

The afterlife will never be one filled with agony, these people say, but simply with quiet joy, inner bliss, and the peaceful and serene knowing of who and what we really are, followed by the ever-expanding expression and experience of this through an ongoing series of physicalizations that are commonly called reincarnations.

This group believes that we did not simply "find" ourselves here on Earth, having had nothing to do with our arrival, but came here quite on purpose, manifesting in physicality with a particular and specific intent that is identical for all of us (the continued evolution of the soul), but singularly experienced in each of us, according to our individuated modes of expression (even as musicians might play the same composition in entirely different ways).

Whichever group one belongs to, far too many humans, when considering their beliefs, will neither concede, nor even acknowledge the *possibility,* that what they believe may not be totally true—and could even be completely mistaken. Their beliefs about God and about life are, they assert, indisputable, irrefutable, and incontestable. These are, they would say, their most wonderful ideas about all of this.

Now none of this would matter a great deal if we all kept our most sacred beliefs to ourselves, not letting them seep into and affect our collective exterior experience. Yet what would be the point of holding beliefs to be sacred if we have no intention of *living them* in our daily lives and *inserting them* into our daily experience?

We see then how many of humanity's spiritual beliefs (including the *non*-belief in God and spirituality) spill over into our politics, our economics, and our social constructions of every kind.

The problem isn't that we carry our most sacred beliefs into the marketplace of ideas. The problem is *what* those sacred beliefs *are*—and the fact that our thoughts about how those viewpoints and understandings should apply in areas of civil law, politics, economics, and social constructions *also* become hardened, indisputable, irrefutable, and incontestable.

It is both the possible inaccuracy of some of our beliefs, and our absolute intransigence as we express them in our public and collective encounters, that is producing Alienation. In our streets. In our public meetings. In our online postings. In our legislative assemblies. In our homes.

(I'm going to capitalize the word "Alienation" throughout

the rest of this discussion, because it is the central, major, and most negatively impacting, civilization-threatening, social contract–dismantling challenge of our time.)

Humans of goodwill everywhere today are begging to know: Is *any* of this improvable, correctable, changeable? Are we in a slide down a slippery slope that cannot be stopped?

The answer to the first question is yes. The answer to the second question is no. But if we want the slide to stop, we're going to have to refuse to continue our continual *refusal*.

8

THE REFUSAL

As noted earlier, our most important beliefs are the beliefs we live by, base our decisions on, rationalize our choices with. They are the lens through which we look, and they determine, to a huge extent, what we see. (We tend to see what we put there before we looked.)

The most sacred of those beliefs for most people are the thoughts and understandings, convictions and notions, that have been embraced and embedded deeply within them regarding what is true about life, about our relationship to each other, about how life itself functions, about who we are and our reason and purpose for being here, about God (including the belief that there *is* no God), and about the ultimate goal of the whole experience we are undergoing on Earth. These particular beliefs are critical, because they fuel the engine of our lives, both collectively and individually.

Given how significant the beliefs are, one would think that people would examine them often, if only to see if their ideas still feel valid and true. Yet most people do not. In fact, the majority of people do exactly the opposite. They don't closely examine their most dearly held beliefs at all. Ever.

Why do so many folks refuse to acknowledge that their beliefs could contain even the slightest error, or that it might be time to change them because times themselves have changed? What is this reluctance about?

It is about where those beliefs came from. For most people that would be those who raised them. Then their extended family—their tribe, their clan, their race, their teachers, models, and elders. Finally, their given religion and their acquired philosophy, their adopted politics, and their individual history. And because these are such significant and personally meaningful sources, much of humanity has found itself stuck in a most unusual place.

This is not a place where we find ourselves stuck in any other area of our collective lives. Not in science, not in technology, not in medicine. Only with regard to our most sacred and important beliefs.

In every other important area of human endeavor there is *something we have been willing to do* that has made those endeavors productive, fruitful, and enormously beneficial. Yet in one area—ironically, the most important area of our lives—our *beliefs* . . . we have *staunchly refused to do it.*

Our willingness to do it in science has resulted in extraordinary discoveries. Our willingness to do it in medicine has resulted in breathtaking advances. Our willingness to do it in technology has resulted in astonishing inventions.

And what *is* it that we have done in *every other area of our lives* that we have adamantly *refused* to do in the one area that is most important—our beliefs?

QUESTION THE PRIOR ASSUMPTION

In science, the very *reason* we have been able to discover something that we did not understand before is that the moment we think we have found an answer, we have been willing to *question the prior assumption.*

In medicine, the very *reason* we have been able to come up with a new cure or a miraculous new procedure is that the moment we think we have found an answer, we have been willing to *question the prior assumption.*

In technology, the very *reason* that we have been able to imagine or conceive of a new tool or a new device is that the moment we think we have found an answer, we have been willing to *question the prior assumption.*

In all of these areas we have held nothing that we *thought* we knew to be so sacred that it cannot even be questioned. It may take us some time, we may do it with some reluctance, yet sooner or later breakthroughs occur, because we have finally questioned the prior assumption.

But not so in the area of our most sacred beliefs. In that area, we are going to hold on to the Original Idea and the First Version of things, no matter what. *This is what we have been told, this is what we know, and this is how it is,* we say.

Now, if we did this in medicine, we would be attempting brain surgery today using a very sharp stick. If we did this in technology, we would be trying to launch a communications satellite using a stack of dynamite. If we did this in science, we would be seeking to unravel the mysteries of the universe using an abacus.

We need now to do with our beliefs what we have done in every other important area of human endeavor. *We need to stop trying to solve modern problems with ancient tools.*

A very wise teacher once said to me, "Who would you have to make wrong in order to get things right?" As long as you need to continue to make your *sources* "right," you may never be able to "right a wrong" in your *world.*

We must give ourselves permission to raise questions about our most sacred beliefs regarding life—and even regarding God. We must be willing to question authority. Indeed, to question The Highest Authority. We must be willing to make the daring decision to *choose God*—in a brand-new way, in a way we may never have done before—or not to. And, most courageous of all, to question what we assume we know *about* God.

So the issue before humankind now is: Do we have the courage to do so? Are we brave enough to consider the possibility that it is our *Prior Assumption* about the entire human encounter that has created the daily struggles and the mounting stress that is so real a part of life on Earth for billions today?

THE ASSUMPTION

The biggest and most damaging assumption about life that most of humanity has refused to question is the Assumption of Separation.

There's a fascinating story that I will share with you in just a bit about how we may have come to that assumption in the first place. But right now, let's explore the most powerful impact in our daily lives of that assumption. It is found in humanity's most prevalent idea about what some people call God.

The assumption is impactful because most people who believe in God (and that is, incidentally, by far the largest number of people on this planet, so this is not unimportant) embrace what could be called a Separation Theology. This is a way of looking at God that says that God is "up there" and we are "down here" and never the twain shall meet, except on Judgment Day, when we'll find out whether our behavior has been sufficiently passable to allow us to return to heaven.

The fact that billions of people hold some version of this idea to be true would, perhaps, not matter too much if it began and ended there, but the challenge with a Separation Theology is that it produces, too often in too many people, a Separation Cosmology. That is, a way of looking at all of life that says that everything is separate from everything else.

This wouldn't be so bad if it were just a point of view, but the challenge with a Separation Cosmology is that it produces, too often in too many people, a Separation Psychology. That is, a psychological viewpoint that says that I am over here and you are over there, and we each have our separate needs and requirements, our separate desires, and, therefore, our separate agendas.

This would also be something we could live with if that was all there was to it, but the challenge with a Separation Psychology is that it produces, too often in too many people, a Separation Sociology. That is, a way of socializing with each other that encourages everyone within human society to join together in separate groups, cultures, nations, religions, political parties, families, and organizations, each serving their own separate interests.

Now we encounter something that we *can't* live with, because a Separation Sociology inevitably produces, too often in too many people, a Separation Pathology. That is, pathological behaviors of self-destruction, engaged in individually and collectively, and producing suffering, conflict, violence, and death—evidenced everywhere on our planet throughout human history.

The idea that everything is separate from everything else is the biggest reason that the world is the way it is today, and the greatest obstacle to the rapid expansion of human potential.

Our Story of Separation is as old as humanity itself. It is fascinating to look at one way it could have become a staple of our culture, by imagining what I call a very possible story.

THE STORY

If you dropped a deck of cards on the floor and then found them lying in perfect order by rank and suit, you would not call that a coincidence. You would call it an impossibility under ordinary circumstances, and conclude that there must be something larger at play.

The same would be true of the Universe. The impeccability of its intricacy and the utter perfection in the way its "cards have fallen" is too flawless to be the result of sheer coincidence. The odds of the cosmos having manifested its mechanics and the sheer wonder of its sentient beings "by accident" or "random chance" are—to use a well-chosen word—astronomical. Clearly, something larger is at play.

The question is, what is It? And what is Its purpose? What, if anything, is Its desire? What, if any, are Its stipulations? What, if anything, does It need from us, want from us, demand from us, command of us, and reprimand us for if we do not meet Its requirements?

These are not small questions. We have been trying to answer them from the beginning of the first moments of our sentience as living beings on the Earth.

What we now call "self-consciousness" probably arose when we began to see or know ourselves individually. Perhaps it was seeing our reflection in a caveside pool that sparked this perception. I could easily imagine it happening this way. We raised a hand to scratch our head and saw the "man in the pool" doing the same thing . . . and soon we began to conceive of "The Self."

We had already noticed that "The Self" was "different" from others. And in our primitive minds, we confused "different from" with "separate from."

The next step in producing the perception of separation came, perhaps, as we sat around the campfire of our clan and found ourselves startled by a sudden flash of lightning in the night sky, followed by a booming clap of thunder.

We looked anxiously around the campfire and asked, with whatever facial and verbal expressions we'd developed, "Did you do that?" When everyone in the clan signaled a panicked "No!" we came to a startling awareness: There Is Something Other Than Us.

This Something Other also seemed, as subsequent events appeared to prove, far more powerful than we were. It could cause wind and rain and violent storms; heat and dry spells that lasted, it felt, forever; a frightening shaking and even an opening of the very ground on which we walked. It could even start fires in the woods all by Itself.

It became clear to us that we needed to find a way to control this Something Other, or our lives would forever be at Its mercy. Yet we could not conceive of or imagine a way that we could do this. We tried everything. We knew we had to find a way to appease the gods.

We didn't call the elements of life "gods," of course. That word came along at a much later time. But we did think of this Something Other as an aspect of our existence that was both powerful and uncontrollable.

We experienced some members of our own clan in exactly the same way, for this was the Time of Brute Strength, when the biggest and the strongest and most brutish among us ran rampant through the collective life of the clan, and always got their way.

We had learned as a species that physical strength was needed for survival, and so the strongest were accorded the highest place in the clan. Efforts were continually made to appease them. They were brought offerings of every kind, from nubile virgins to plentiful food to beautiful things from the richness of the earth.

Once, when the most brutish in our clan became more sullen and angry than usual because of an unending drought and the sacrifices it imposed on him and the whole clan, we joined others in our small group to do whatever we could think of to calm him, lest he take out his anger on us—which he had done before.

We threw a campside "party" for him, sang and did dances for him. Someone in the group tore a dying branch from a nearby tree and shook it as part of his dance, its dry leaves making a rhythmic sound matching his gyrations as he twirled around the fire.

As it happens, at that exact moment the skies opened up, and a sudden hard rain drenched the site. Everyone was shocked! And given the limited intellectual development of the clan at that time, the Dance with the Branch was credited with having produced the water from the sky and ending the drought.

A way had been found to please and appease the "Something Other," whatever it was, that produced the drought and produced the rain! A way had been found to get that Something Other to do what we had been hoping for! All of us were excited! The "rain man" was elevated to a position of high status, second only to the Leader of the Clan.

And so The One Most Clever stood, from that day forward, alongside The One Most Brutish. As well, "rituals," and a separate class within the clan, were created.

The clan believed that the Dance with the Branch by the Rain Man created rain, and so the dance *did* create rain more often than not as time went on. And this was hardly a coincidence. Metaphysics being was it is, the *belief* of the clan members, all holding the same idea in the same way, had the power to produce the outcome.

In short, the formula for creation worked! The metaphysical process—whether modern or ancient—often produces in physicality whatever is fervently believed by a collective. And yes, even by a strong-minded individual. In that first instance around the cave dwellers' campfire, it was no doubt the clan's ongoing, fervent hope, its deeply earnest wish, that the drought would end, which generated the result.

But the coincidence of the rain falling at the exact moment the noisy dance was performed could not be ignored. So the clan drew an inaccurate conclusion. The earliest humans were dealing with the alchemy of the universe without knowing it. They attributed the rain to the dance and the Rain Man who performed it, rather than to their own thoughts, their own most urgently felt desire. It was his power, not theirs, his ritual, not their collective energy. They had nothing to do with it.

Thus was born . . . religion. And within the human culture, religion has become a long-standing tradition.

THE TRADITION

There is no historical record, nor even an educated guess of cosmologists, which suggests that the preceding narrative has any basis in fact. The story is all of my imagining. It was an insight I received when thinking deeply about how things could have happened.

And while the entire story may be inaccurate, I believe that either this, or something very similar to it, might very well actually be what occurred in the early life of human beings, and how we placed firmly in our traditions our sense of separation, our sense of Something Other, and our sense that there might be, after all is said and done, a way of *controlling* or *influencing* that Something Other.

And as humanity became more sophisticated in its understandings, the species sought a more sophisticated way of accessing that control and influence by trying to "appease the gods" . . . and, much later, of working to please the single Higher Power that humans ultimately decided must surely exist.

About that much we were right. There *is* a Higher Power,

which humans have referred to by various names throughout history—and to this very day.

A person called Colin wrote me an email several years ago providing me with what he said was a non-exhaustive list of the names given to the gods that various human societies have believed in at one time or another. I never got Colin's last name, but I am grateful to him for the research.

The names for God on Colin's list include: Adonai, Ægir, Akshar, Alfar, Allah, Amaterasu, An, Angus, Anshar, Anu, Anubis, Aphrodite, Apollo, Apsu, Ares, Artemis, Atehna, Ashur, Ataegina, Aten, Attis, Atum, Azura Mazda, Bacchus, Balder, Bast, Bes, Belenos, Benzaiten, Beyla, Bil, Bishamonten, Bragi, Brama, Brigid, Byggvir, Ceres, Cupid, Cybele, Dagda, Dagr, Daikoku, Damkina. Dana, Demeter, Deus, Diana, Dionysus, Disir, Divine Mother, Divinity, Ea, Ebisu, Eir, Ekankar, El-Gabal, Elohim, Elves, Endovelicus, Enki, Enlil, Eos, Eostre, Epona, Ereshkigal, Eris, Forseti, Freya, Freyr, Frigga, Fukurokuju, Fulushou, Gaia, Ganesh, Geb, God, Hadad, Hapi, Hari, Hathor, Heget, Heimdall, Hekate, Helios, Hephaestus, Hera, Hermes, Herne, Hestia, Hoenir, Holda, Horus, Hotei, Hretha, Idunn, Imhotep, Inanna, Inari, Indra, Inti, Invictus, Ishtar, Isis, Izanagi, Izanami, Janus, Jehovah, Jord, Juno, Jupiter, Jurojin, Khepry, Khnum, Kingu, Kishar, Kon, Krishna, Lofn, Loki, Lord, Lugh, Maahes, Ma'at, Mahesh, Maia, Mama Cocha, Mama Quilla, Manco Capac, Manitou, Marduk, Mars, Mathilde, Menhit, Mercury, Minerva, Mithras, Mitra, Mon, Mont, Mummu, Nabu, Nammu, Nanna, Naunet, Nehalennia, Neith, Nephthys, Neptune, Nergal, Nerthus, Ninhursag,

Ninlil, Nintu, Njord, Norns, Nott, Nunurta, Nut, Odin, Ormuzd, Osiris, Pachacamac, Pan, Parameshwar, Plutus, Poseidon, Proserpina, Ptah, Purush, Purushottam, Quetzalcoatl, Ra, Radha Soami, Ram, Rama, Ran, Runesocesius, Saga, Saxnot, Sekhmnet, Selene, Set, Shamash, Shef, Shiva, Sif, Sin, Siofn, Skadi, Snotra, Sobek, Sol, Susanoo, Syn, Tefnut, Tengu, Theos, Thor, Thoth, Thuno, Tiamat, Tir, Tlaloc, Tsukiyomi, Tyr, Ull, Uranus, Utu, Vali, Var, Varuna, Venus, Vesta, Vidar, Vishnu, Vor, Vulcan, Weyland, Woden, Yahweh, Zaramama, Zeus.

I printed all those names here so that you would see that I'm not exaggerating when I say that this embracing of a Higher Power by humanity has become a tradition, and has been going on for a long time. A very, *very* long time.

Whatever name we use to refer to It, there is little dispute that the largest number of beings on this planet continue to believe in a Higher Power. Yet our idea *about* that Higher Power—that It exists as "something other" than us, or "some other" version of life—is what larger and larger numbers of people are beginning to question.

Many people are beginning to see that the earliest story we told ourselves about The Power Greater Than Us has indeed created a Separation Theology that has produced what could be, after all is said and done, humanity's biggest misunderstanding.

12

THE MISUNDERSTANDING

The biggest misunderstanding of our species may be this: We think we know what we're doing here.

Our thought about what should be our prime focus on Earth is based, perhaps not in whole, but surely in very large part, on the ideas that so many people hold about God—including the idea that there is no such thing as God.

To place this into an easy-to-get-a-handle-on context, let's take a second look at how people tend to fall into categories around this, because it's easily observable that the category into which people fall has a great deal to do with what they understand life's purpose and their agenda to be.

Billions of people—you'll remember them as Group One—will tell you that the most important thing they are doing here, when all is said and done, is working to get to Heaven, or Paradise, or Elysium. They see life as a "test." A "trial," if you will, to see if they are worthy, or can *render* themselves worthy, of returning to The Divine in the afterlife.

According to these billions, humans have souls, which are loosely defined as their "spiritual selves." The common doctrine embraced by these billions is that God separated souls from Himself because of His displeasure with the first of their kind—whose sinful ways they are said to have inherited.

The mythical story of Adam and Eve being cast out of Paradise has been repeated in one form or another in several cultures, each of which teaches some version of The Great Separation. In some Korean homes, to offer just one of many examples an anthropologist might provide, the story of Mago's Garden is told.

This tale speaks of a Deity who created a Paradise and then placed in it human creations of different colors, like flowers in a beautiful garden. Because of their differences, however, these creatures fought amongst themselves, and so, in Her disappointment and anger, Mago banished Her creations from the Garden.

She separated them and sent them to different places upon the Earth, telling them that they may return to the Garden only when they learned to exist together harmoniously.

According to the continuation of this story, the people of different colors on Earth have been trying to find a way to do so ever since.

So it is that cultural stories around the world preach about the need of all souls to get back into God's good graces if they wish to spend eternity in Nirvana.

What we are doing here on Earth, those in Group One believe, is seeking salvation.

Others, holding no such theological view (and in many cases no theology at all), may embrace the assumption that there is something else we are here to do.

These people—they're in Group Two—believe that life is exactly, and nothing more than, what it appears to be: a random series of events, having no particular meaning or larger-scale purpose, to which we hope we can respond in a way which causes the least amount of damage to ourselves and others. Humanity's chief goal, then, is survival, followed by enjoyment, meaningful contribution and purposeful achievement, and, of course, the care of loved ones.

When our end comes, Group Two believes, there is nothing hereafter, and so, nothing that we will find afterlife benefit in focusing our here-and-now energies upon. There is no overarching goal or purpose other than living life in the best way one can, moment to moment, using one's own definition of how that is defined and demonstrated, and one's own measure of how well one has succeeded.

The central question for humanity now is: What if both Group One and Group Two are embracing understandings that are wholly or partially inaccurate? What if The Actuality lies somewhere between these groups and the ideas offered by Group Three (described in Chapter 7, for those of you who want to look back to review them)—ideas that few in either of the first two groups are willing to even consider, much less seriously explore?

The result could be that billions of people may be walking around with very limited ideas of what they are doing on Earth, little or no concept that there may be a purpose in life other than what they have thought of, little or no awareness of what could be their own True Nature, and little or no understanding of a possible alternative relationship with the rest of the cosmos—not to mention its Source.

Could it be that the world as it now is, with its widespread dysfunctions, travesties, and terrorism, is a reflection of this limited viewpoint? Could it be that what we are seeing as we look at our world is a mirror of some incomplete understandings?

Those misunderstandings could explain why, while we call ourselves an advanced civilization, billions of people—that is to say, *enormous* slices of our total population—are nevertheless suffering dreadfully and needlessly (as evidenced by the sobering statistics found in Chapter 4).

Every thinking person would surely want to know: How has it come to pass that things have come to this?

That is a lyrically put question that surely must arise in the heart of every compassionate being. Surely you have felt it in your own heart more than once in recent times.

How has it *come to pass* that things have *come to this?*

The answer is that we think we must obey what we have completely misidentified as our basic instinct.

13

THE INSTINCT

It is a telling and fascinating fact that in this, the first quarter of the 21st century, most humans continue to believe that survival is the basic instinct.

Our species has believed this for thousands of years, and the majority of us still feel that whatever it takes to survive needs to be considered first and foremost in nearly all political, economic, and societal interactions. (Even in our own households, our interactions are often about surviving the moment.)

We don't want to have to hurt anybody to survive . . . but we'll do it—emotionally or even physically—if we need to.

It is the supreme irony that our determination to make survival our continual priority *is what causes our survival to be continually threatened.*

That has never been more sadly in evidence than it is today, with Alienation producing moments when world leaders regularly announce their ability to annihilate each other's countries, when the discontented and disconnected are engaging in self-indulgent rampages killing innocent people, and when fear and anger starkly divide a species whose best defense against all that besets it is unity of purpose and action.

The argument in favor of survival is that it is observed to be the basic instinct of many life-forms. It's what makes flowers turn toward the sun, birds fly to warmer climates, turtles recede into their shells, and rattlesnakes rattle.

It turns out, however, that the basic instinct of human beings is *not* survival. It is something quite different. Something *altogether* different.

If survival were your basic instinct, you would run away from the burning building when you hear a baby crying on the second floor. But you don't. You run *into* the building, because in that moment your survival is not the issue.

If survival were your basic instinct, you would step away from the person holding a gun on your beloved. But you don't. You stand *between* that person and your beloved, because in that moment your survival is not the issue.

If survival were your basic instinct, you would drive away from the car on the side of the road with the engine on fire and a man frozen in shock behind the wheel. But you don't. You stop your car, run over to the other vehicle, snap the driver out of his stupor, and risk your life to pull him out of the car before it explodes, because in that moment your survival is not the issue.

Something deep inside of you, something you cannot describe or name, moves you in such moments to obey *humanity's* basic instinct.

People who have demonstrated courage by stepping into life-threatening situations rarely describe themselves as courageous when interviewed by the media later. No, they demur, "I just did what anybody would do."

They say they simply acted on instinct. *And they did.* What they may not have known is that their basic instinct has nothing to do with survival.

Perhaps to their own surprise, their actions *defied* survival. Yet they had no fear and no hesitation—not even a *thought* of either—at the time, because Who They Really Are knew that survival was not at issue.

In what I have come to call life's Burning Building Moments, very few of us have questions about whether we will survive. As we look back on such moments later, we realize that the only question that's really important to our soul is not whether we will live twenty more years or twenty more minutes, but *how?*

What shall be the signature of my life? What shall be the chief motivator of my days and nights? What is my *raison d'être,* as the French call it—my reason for being—and how do my actions actuate and actualize that?

And in such moments of self-exploration, the Mind and the Soul answer as One.

The basic instinct of human beings is the spontaneous expression of the best within us. What has poetically been called The Better Angels of our Nature.

But what *is* our Nature?

We've heard the phrase "it's human nature" all of our lives. But what *is* that? What is the True Nature of our species?

This is the question of the hour. Now, more than ever on this planet, the asking and answering of this question is our biggest challenge.

14

THE CHALLENGE

We have a decision to make. We have to decide Who and What We Are. This is the most important decision our species will ever make. It is the Daring Decision. It is the only decision we need to make to solve forever the problem of our Alienation.

It is imperative that we make this decision now. Not in six decades, or sixty decades. Now. We simply—forgive me for being a bit emphatic, but we simply can't go on like this, playing the fiddle while Rome burns, or standing by idly and offering no comment on the emperor's new clothes. We have to *stop fiddling around and just tell the naked truth.*

We're in trouble here. The rapidly spreading *us* vs. *them* mentality is tearing at the fabric of humanity. We are being called upon by life itself to ask: What *is* our True Nature? What do we mean when we say "it's human nature" to act in a certain way?

And is human nature evolving or devolving? In which direction is our culture moving? Are we becoming more civilized, more humane, more loving, more caring, more tolerant, more accepting, more understanding, more forgiving, more open-hearted and open-armed and more compassionate . . . or less? What does your observation tell you?

To me, it's clear that the choice before us now is the choice between evolution and devolution, and that this choice is being made now—largely by default. The process is going on right in front of our eyes.

The time for decisiveness is at hand. And what we have to decide, I repeat, is Who and What We Are. As individuals and as a collective. And we are being challenged now to make the right choice, not continue to make the wrong choice.

By "right" and "wrong" I don't mean morally right or wrong, I mean what is the right direction to take, based on where we say we want to be going as a species. In that context, what is beneficial and what is detrimental? What "works" and what "does not work"?

We've been choosing what does not work for too long. We've been selecting that which is detrimental even more in recent times.

Look around you.

The challenge for us has been that we have not seen the matter of Who and What We Are as something that is optional. We've seen it as an observation, not a decision; as something we notice, not something we choose.

Who and What We Are is, many of us have told ourselves, a *given*. It is what is *so*. And in fact this is true. It *is* "what is so." Yet what if what is *so* is not what we *thought* was so? If we imagine human nature to be other than what human nature actually *is*, wouldn't the entire human experience be deformed, distressed, and distorted?

Hmmm . . . caught the news lately?

The decision that is ours, then, is whether what *is* so is "so" for *us*. That is, we have to decide whether we believe it or not. We have to decide if it is *really* so.

There is a device by which we can make this assessment about *all* that people tell us is "so." There is an objective measure that we can use with every one of our beliefs. That device, that measure, is a simple but fair evaluation, an honest appraisal, of the events, situations, circumstances, conditions, and outcomes in our lives.

This can be narrowed down to one word: results.

Here are some ways this measuring device may be used.

Judging by results and using fair appraisal, do the doctrines and dogmas about God and about life offered by the world's religions appear to be what is *so* when we look at how effective they have been in helping us to live together in peace and harmony? Or does it appear that there may be something *still to learn* on this subject?

Judging by results and using fair appraisal, do the theories and the concepts of the world's political and economic systems appear to be what is *so* when we look at how effectively those systems have created more harmony and greater financial security for us all? Or does it appear that there may be something *still to learn* on this subject?

Judging by results and using fair appraisal, do the most glowing descriptions and the highest assessments of the world's Internet system appear to be what is *so* when we look at how social media platforms have met the goal of generating more connectedness and togetherness between people? Or does it appear that there may be something *still to learn* on this subject?

Now, let's apply this measure to the question at hand.

Judging by results and using fair appraisal, do the ideas that you hold about Who and What You Are appear to be what is *so* when you look at how well those ideas have produced peace, joy, security, happiness, love, full expression, and fulfillment in your daily life, and in life around the world? Or does it appear that there may be something *still to learn* on this subject?

Might it be beneficial to make a new decision about what is "so" *for* us regarding what is "so" *about* us? Is it really healthy—to say nothing of being *workable*—to have made that decision by default, by virtue of having belonged to a certain and particular Group?

You can make that new decision right now. Consciously, not Groupfully. I just made up a word right there to describe how so many people make their decisions. But this is not just any decision. This is the Daring Decision that your heart is leaping to make, that your soul is urging you to make, that your mind is yearning to make. This is a decision that can put you on a new path.

If you've already made this decision, let's do it again. To confirm it. And to clarify what you've actually chosen.

We are talking here about choosing your identity, and there are two aspects to this decision. The first has to do with Who You Are and the second has to do with What You Are.

Put into question form, the decision regarding all humans comes down to this:

1. Are we temporary physical beings, or Spiritual Beings Manifesting Physically?
2. Are we completely separate entities, or One Essence Manifesting Individually?

Basically, the question is: "What *is* our True Nature?" It is about this that life is now urging us to make a choice.

15

THE CHOICE

Many people have not thought a great deal about the first of the two elements that make up their Identity. Looking at it now, let's see which of the choices that life has placed before us is most likely to produce the experience that you desire.

Choice A: You could conceive of yourself as an exclusively Physical Being. That is, as a biological creature whose life was initiated as the result of a biological process engaged in by two other biological creatures, and whose life is terminated when one or more of its critical biological processes cease to function beneficially.

If you embrace this notion of yourself, you will likely see yourself as having the same connection to the larger processes of life as any other biological life-form, but no more.

You will understand yourself to be, like all other physical life-forms, impacted by life's daily events, conditions, and circumstances, but with limited ability to influence those events, conditions, and circumstances in advance. You could *react* to all of them, but you could *create* only some of them—actually, the smallest number—based on your talents and abilities, intelligence and determination, and, to a large degree, your good fortune.

You could create more *life* (all physical life-forms carry the biological capacity to recreate more of themselves), but you could not create what life *does,* or how it "shows up" in any given moment except, as just noted, in a few limited ways.

Further, as a Physical Being you will most likely see yourself as having a somewhat limited ability to produce an always predictable and inevitably desirable response to the events and conditions arising in life.

You could do this occasionally, of course, but you might more often observe yourself as a creature whose responses are ruled by prior data and instinct, culture, environment, upbringing, experience, training, education, and habit, and whatever natural resources that your biology and your history bring you.

You will see yourself as having more resources than a turtle, because your biology and history have gifted you with more. You will see yourself as having more resources than a butterfly, because your biology and history have gifted you with more. Yet your biology and history are basically what you will see yourself as having in terms of resources.

Your creativity and ingenuity would be part of your biological (in this case, mental) resources that could in some cases overcome your history, but you may find it to be true that environment, background, previous experience, and culture play a major role in your responses—particularly your initial responses—to events more often than not.

In summary, as a Physical Being you will most likely see

yourself as having to deal with life day-by-day pretty much as it comes, with perhaps the smallest amount of what could be called "control," based on advance planning, etc., and you would know that at any minute anything could go wrong—and often does.

Finally, as a Physical Being you will most likely experience that you are here (on Earth, that is) for no reason in particular—and certainly no reason that you had anything to do with.

You might then feel the necessity and the impulse, sooner or later, to decide *for yourself* what your reason for being is going to be, i.e., whether the primary focus and concern of your time here should be on the most desired expression of your gifts and talents, your occupation, your income or possessions, your achievements or place in society, your family or lifestyle, or perhaps in some ways all of the above, and how you are succeeding in producing your desired outcomes.

Choice B: You could conceive of yourself as a Spiritual Being Manifesting Physically.

You will then have a basis for considering the possibility that you have powers and abilities beyond those of one who is limited to being a Physical Being only. You might see these powers as transcending basic physicality and its laws.

You will then have a basis for considering the possibility that these powers and abilities give you collaborative control over the exterior elements of your individual and collective life, and complete control over the interior elements.

This would mean that you have the ability to create your own reality, inasmuch as what is "real" to you is firmly based on your singular interior experience of the collaborative outward creations of your life.

Also, as a Spiritual Being, you will have a basis for considering the possibility that you are here on Earth for a spiritual reason, and that you moved into "physicalization" at your own behest.

You might see your purpose in doing so as having little to do directly with your occupation or career, your income or possessions, your achievements or place in society, or *any* of the exterior conditions or circumstances of your life, but mostly with a spiritual agenda, a more essential path.

You will also notice that how well you do in achieving your larger purpose—that is, how you create the interior experiences and energies of your life—can have an effect on your exterior life. You will then have a foundation for considering the possibility that your *interior* energy can actually generate events and conditions in your *exterior* reality. But it will all be based on what will wind up being your life's biggest decision.

16

THE DECISION

The question regarding the second aspect of humanity's True Nature is: Are we completely Separate Entities or One Essence Manifesting Individually?

The implications of our answer to this question are profound. Let's explore the decision here and see which option is most likely to produce the experiences you desire.

Option A: You could conceive of yourself as a Separate Entity. That is, as a single unit among billions of single units on our planet.

If you see yourself in this way, you will experience being physically "other than" and disconnected from the 7+ billion people in the world, and emotionally detached from all but the tiniest percentage of them. You will see yourself as disengaged from their agendas, and not aligned with their intentions or motives unless they directly coincide with your own.

You will most likely experience yourself as unfastened from the future of others if you do not see their future as in some way affecting or impacting your personal experience, and you may feel disjointed, at best, in efforts you may pursue to functionally link your future with that of the largest portion of humanity in any meaningful or effective way.

You will also most likely experience yourself not only as being, more or less and more often than not, "on your own," but also openly *competing* with others in an "every man for himself" society within a "to the victor go the spoils" culture.

Win or lose, this could cause you to feel increasingly isolated, particularly from those members of your society with whom you appear to have little in common, and especially from those with whom you flat out disagree.

And if your disagreement with certain others grows to severe proportions—owing to the fact that, in seeing yourself as a separate creature, you focus most heavily on your separate needs and interests, separate desires, and a separate agenda with separate objectives—your sense of isolation could turn into an experience of desolation, especially if your needs and desires are not met. This could produce a level of estrangement that leads to Alienation.

You might find yourself, as an antidote to feeling isolated in your Alienation, joining a group or movement with other people who feel as you do. And should the disagreement of many such groups become vitriolic or violent, Alienation can become a worldwide societal problem, dismantling the connecting structures of our global community.

It not only *can,* it is. Right now. As you are reading this.

We are not even surprised anymore when the impact and the effect of our species' growing Alienation is evidenced and announced in headlines blasting from online news sites onto computer screens around the world.

Many people have become completely desensitized to this, resulting in the planetary agony of apathy. Those who are not desensitized are brought to their knees every day, asking—begging—God or Life or *something* to wake our species *up,* to shake us out of the communal slumber that has produced the nightmare of our collective global reality.

(This is, of course, where you come in.)

Option B: You could conceive of yourself as One Essence Manifesting Individually.

If you see yourself in this way, you will most likely feel connected both in a physical way as well as an emotional way with all humans—and in an energetic way with every expression of life.

You will see yourself as part of the Body Human, in no way detached from the other 7+ billion people in the world, but engaged with their current agendas and aligned with their present intentions and motives out of your observation that they coincide with your own at the highest level.

You will most likely also experience yourself as firmly fastened to the future of others, seeing clearly that it, too, coincides with your own, and you will then work with sincerity and commitment to combine your future with that of the larger group in a meaningful way.

You will experience yourself as joining with others in an "all for one and one for all" society, with an "all true benefits are mutual" culture, producing the remarkable outcomes in individual and collective lives that naturally arise from such a mutually held outlook.

This will cause you to feel increasingly unified with other

members of your species, realizing that surely the majority hold the most important things in common. You will see that differences do not have to produce divisions, that contrasts do not have to produce conflicts, that disagreements do not have to produce disaffection, that variance does not have to produce violence, and that proponents do not have to become opponents.

You will know experientially (and not merely understand conceptually) that "individuation" does not automatically equate to "separation"—seeing evidence in your own hand, where you will observe that your fingers, though individual in size, appearance, and function, are in no way separate from your hand, nor from your body, nor, therefore, from each other.

You will experience a deep awareness that all lives are intertwined, that what you do for another you do for yourself, and that what you fail to do for another you fail to do for yourself, because there is, in Ultimate Reality, no one else except extensions of yourself, manifesting in differing form.

This will cause you to replace competition with cooperation, Alienation with affirmation, and separation with unification, allowing the human race to act as One in facing and meeting its challenges.

17

THE MAJORITY

Here's something interesting: Looking at the first aspect of our True Nature—Who We Are—it is clear that the majority of Earth's people already see themselves as Spiritual Beings Manifesting Physically. This is the result of their belief in God and in a life after death. They often refer to the part of themselves that moves through physical life with the body as the "soul" or spirit, psyche, atman, anima, etc.

The challenge is that many people may have come to see themselves in this way automatically, without really questioning it, as a result of their default mechanism having "kicked in" if they grew up within, or came later in life to accept, the story told by many of the world's organized religions.

This means that they may accept beliefs about their Identity as souls that may not translate in any practical or functional way to their day-to-day behaviors.

This is, of course, not always the case, and huge numbers of the faithful no doubt express the highest values of their religions in their daily life. Yet many do so out of fear that to not do so—that is, to commit certain sins of omission or commission—is to invite condemnation and eternal damnation.

(Please don't think I'm making this up, or exaggerating. I'm not. May I offer one example? I was taught in my Catholic childhood that it was a mortal sin [i.e., a very serious, grave offense against God] to miss going to Mass and receiving Communion on any Sunday, or on a Holy Day of Obligation. [The Church puts out a calendar to let you know when those are.] And the Church teaches that if you die with the offense of having missed Mass on your soul, you go straight to hell. We're not talking about purgatory here. We're talking about hell.

Mind you, I did not say I was taught that one goes to hell for murdering somebody, or for the rape of a child, or for stealing another's life savings. I said that God will send you to hell for *missing Mass on Sunday* if you died with that sin on your soul. [That is, if you did not have a chance to go to Confession and receive Absolution before you died.]

Would that make a child look both ways at the corner? Let me *tell* you . . .

Has the Church loosened up on this stance since I was a child in the 1950s? No. I checked. I wanted to make sure. Priests still teach that it's a "mortal sin." Sickness and physical inability [care of a child, needing to work, being infirm] are the only acceptable excuses. You either go to church or go to hell. No fear motive here. [Ahem]

So no, I wasn't exaggerating or making something up about this business of fear being a motivator for many people following the doctrines of their religion.)

There are others who choose to see themselves as a spirit, or soul, out of love. Simple, pure love for The Divine as they conceive of it. This choice arises not out of fear or as a reflex, but out of a confident acceptance and embracing of their spiritual reality—which, for many, defines God as a Loving Father and themselves as spiritual offspring.

Finally, there are those people who see themselves as Spiritual Beings Manifesting Physically not as an outgrowth of any specific religious doctrine, but out of a personal hope that physical life is not all there is, a yearning that their identities not cease to exist after death, and a desire for life in the physical body to be about more than simply survival, security, and success. It is far more attractive, reassuring, and comforting to them to embrace the notion that they are not merely physical, biological, or chemical creatures.

Whatever a person's reason for accepting the notion that she or he has and is a soul, this idea, when fully embraced, is a choice that may be more beneficial than not to our species.

If and when the idea is misused as a basis on which to judge, condemn, or mistreat others, this would, of course, not be true. But if the idea is held with a loving energy, if it comforts people and motivates people to act in many positive ways, it could reasonably be seen even by those who view it as an illusion as doing less harm than good.

Deciding that we are merely and simply biological creatures without a soul or any connection to any other power in the Universe, spiritual or otherwise, could be seen, on the other hand, as limiting on many levels.

The possibility of us experiencing the kind of life of which we have all dreamed would, for instance, most likely be seen as more a matter of only hard work and chance rather than hard work and chance *combined with* prayer or positive thinking or intention. And the motivation to "live the good life" could wind up being reduced for some to an almost embarrassingly hedonistic application of Freud's Pleasure Principle.

Yet while defining ourselves as Spiritual Beings Manifesting Physically could help some members of humanity to rise above life choices having only sybaritic value, it can also—as just noted—lead to embracing beliefs that separate and alienate if it results in the formation of groups that declare themselves to be "better" than other groups, and whose members judge others—and even kill others—because they claim that the "others" belong to the "wrong" group (sometimes called "infidels").

We see, then, that even if we decide that we are Spiritual Beings Manifesting Physically, this is in and of itself no guarantee of generating wonderful outcomes for humanity, and is only one part—and the smaller of the two parts at that—of the solution to humanity's alarmingly expanding problem of estrangement. If we are to escape the consequences of runaway Alienation, both aspects of humanity's True Nature will need to be embraced in combination.

18

THE COMBINATION

It is embracing the *combination* of the two aspects of humanity's True Nature that offers a solution to humanity's biggest problem.

This is so because if we decide that *Who* We Are Is a Spiritual Being Manifesting Physically, and at the same time decide that *What* We Are Is One Essence Manifesting Individually (in other words, if we decide that we are both a Spiritual Being and One Being), we can begin to transmogrify the energy that produces Alienation.

Holding such a dual understanding and making it part of our expression of life will make it virtually impossible for us to duplicate the actions and choices of those with whom we disagree. We will simply lose the desire to meet violence with violence, anger with anger, injustice with injustice, injury with injury, or Alienation with Alienation. It will suddenly make no sense to us.

It will become apparent to us that Albert Einstein was right when he said that we cannot solve our problems with the same thinking we used when we created them. We will all be clear that we have to *think in a new way.*

When we see ourselves as One Essence Manifesting Individually, any arising feeling of Alienation will be replaced by a greater tolerance as we remember moments in our own lives when *we* engaged in choices, decisions, or behaviors with which *others* disagreed—and which, often, even we disapproved of ourselves, later.

This shift from Alienation to toleration will likely not occur in everyone's life overnight, but with the passage of time, more and more of us will begin to recognize more and more of ourselves in more and more of each other.

Even then we will not have eliminated all differences between us, but it can mean that we will erase all willingness to have those differences create isolation and desolation, which could only arise out of a thought of complete emotional, physical, or spiritual separation.

It will, to put all this plainly and simply, no longer be *comfortable* for us to endure trading the hopeful potential that the idea of Oneness places before humanity for the empty promise that our species' idea of Separation has dangled in front of us for so long without ever delivering anything but ephemeral and constantly evaporating happiness.

When the largest number of us make the daring decision to fully embrace *both* aspects of our True Nature (Spiritual Being/ One Being), our species will have freed itself at last from the millennia-long effects of the beliefs, misunderstandings, and insanities that arose from its *Prior Assumption*.

Even just dropping the idea held by many that we are nothing more than highly sophisticated mammals would strikingly alter the personal perspective of those who hold such a thought, offering them a dramatically expanded rationale for their daily choices and decisions.

But *combining* the belief that we are spiritual beings with a belief in our oneness as the central tenets of our cultural narrative would not only change *individual* perspectives, but would, once it reached critical mass, beneficially alter the entire global landscape.

The way we do politics, and the *reason* we do politics, would change. The way we do business, and the *reason* we do business, would change. The way we educate our offspring, and the *reason* we educate our offspring, would change.

The way we create our social constructions and conventions, and the *reason* we create our social constructions and conventions, would change. The way we experience our spirituality, and the *reason* we experience our spirituality, would change.

All of this would occur because our motivations, our intentions, our objectives, and our interactions would be altered at every level. Thus, our relationships—nation-with-nation, religion-with-religion, race-with-race, conservative-with-liberal, man-with-woman, straight-with-gay, young-with-old—would become civil at last.

Our problem of Alienation, our idea that violence is a legitimate means of addressing differences, our condition of insufficiency and our unnecessary suffering endured by billions . . . all of this and more would disappear from the Earth, dissolved by new ideas of ourselves that would induce the abandonment of our most damaging self-concepts.

Does this mean we would create a life on Earth without a single concern or challenge of any kind? No. Of course not.

Adopting the idea that we are Spiritual Beings/One Being is not about creating a science-fiction-esque utopian society. But we *can* create a planetary community of far more loving, peaceful, safe, and joyous people, thriving and not constantly struggling, relaxed and not continually straining, celebrating and not endlessly competing or opposing.

Yet if enough early adopters to create critical mass are to embrace the awareness of our True Nature, the idea that we actually *are* Spiritual Beings/One Being will have to make sense to more of us. It's only natural that we would have some curiosities about this business of us all having "souls," and of our "souls" all being in some way united, or conjoined.

There are questions that it is important to explore if one is to form a solid basis or foundation upon which to build a new idea about one's identity, embracing the *combination* of Who and What We Are in fullness. So these are not idle curiosities.

19

THE CURIOSITIES

Fair question time.

If we really are Spiritual Beings Manifesting Physically, where does one soul end and another begin? Is the soul sharply defined and abruptly edged, identifiable by its limits and shape, as is the body?

If two souls hover together in the firmament, is there is a space where the first soul exists and the second soul exists? If so, *what's between them?* What is the substance that separates them?

Could it be that there is *no* substance that separates them, but only a substance that *connects* them—being simply a different vibration of the Same Substance of Which They Are Made?

When you walk from one room of your house into another, where, precisely, does the air of the first room end and the air of the second begin? At the exact nanosecond that the clock strikes midnight, is it the end of one day or the start of another?

What is this place in Time and Space called "both/and"? What happened to "either/or"?

Could it be that when the energy that I call the Essential Essence is coalesced, differentiated, or delineated, we call it a "soul," and that when it is simply Present in an undifferentiated, non-localized, non-concentrated form, we call it All That Is?

Could it be that the soul is *both* Singular *and* Plural? Could it be that it is both permeable and impermeable, unduplicated in its singularity (there are no two snowflakes alike—and no two souls alike), and yet duplicating at the most fundamental level The Singularity Itself?

Could it be that the soul is receiving energy from all around it, and sending energy *to* all around it?

Could it be that what we call "life" is nothing more (and, miracle of miracles, nothing less) than a constant, never-ending process of energy exchange between all the elements of life? Is the mechanism that runs the cosmos the same as the mechanism that runs life in all of its forms—even its sub-molecular form? Is the "system" in which we live a System operating on a Singular Energy that permeates everyone, and is therefore useable by everyone?

Could it be that God (life's Pure, Undifferentiated Energy) was always intended to be used to serve *our* purposes, rather than we being used to serve God's? Or, to be more complete with this thought, that the two are actually one, since *we* are all One, and we just don't know it?

What if God's job is not to tell us what to do, but to empower *us* to do what *we* want to do? Could this be *why the world is the way it is?*

Is it possible that God is empowering us to make our collective choices, giving us the freedom to evolve or devolve as we wish? If we don't want a world in which 653 children die every hour of starvation, do we not have the power to change that through collective action, and with our collective resources? If we don't want a world in which 1.7 billion people do not have access to a drop of clean water, do we not have the power to change that through collective action, and with our collective resources? If we do not want a world in which 1.6 billion people do not have electricity, and 2.5 billion—a third of the human race—still live without toilets, do we not have the power to change that through collective action, and with our collective resources?

It is our species that permits these and other conditions of our collective suffering to exist. God has given us the power to collectively alter these conditions and elevate our civilization to new levels. We are simply not choosing to use that power. If we did, we could change things easily. If we can send a man to the moon, if we can decode the human genome, if we can clone sheep and other mammals (and soon, humans), we can stop 650+ children an hour from dying of starvation. We can stop *all* human-preventable suffering. We simply have to embrace Who We Really Are.

Does this all sound too fanciful, too improbable, or too contradictory to our present orthodoxy to fit into humanity's current thinking?

Dare we think—and dare we actually *say*—that *this* is what we don't fully understand about ourselves, about life, and yes, about God . . . *the understanding of which would change everything?*

That, for sure, is a big dare.

20

THE DARE

It was George Bernard Shaw who observed: "All great truths begin as blasphemies."

If we accept and embrace the combined declaration that all humans are Spiritual Beings Manifesting Physically *and* One Essence Manifesting Individually, we are faced with the logical, if daring, conclusion that all of us are, in *fact,* part of each other.

For some, that's challenging enough. But the logic extends further. The decision would necessarily also declare that, if there is only a Singular Essence in all the Universe and if we see Divinity *as* that Originating and Essential Essence, then all of us must be, as well, a part of what we call God.

This, then, is what is meant by *choosing God.* By deciding to define and experience ourselves both as a Spiritual Being and as One Being, we are choosing to declare that Divinity exists in us, as us, and through us. And that is daring indeed.

For some, such a declaration would seem to border on blasphemy. (Or to cross that border.)

It can be extremely difficult for some people to imagine or accept that God and we are One, that each of us is, in effect, a

Singularization of The Singularity, an Individuation of Divinity. So I want to offer an analogy that helped me, when I first encountered it, bring this huge idea down to something my mind could more easily grapple with.

Consider that we are, to God, as a wave is to the Ocean. The wave arises *from* the Ocean, and expresses itself *as* the Ocean in individuated form, then recedes back *into* the Ocean, to arise and express again in another way in another moment. The Ocean is never not *within* the wave. It *is* the wave, manifesting as An Expression of Itself.

In the same way, we arise *from* The Divine, and express ourselves *as* The Divine in individuated form, then recede back *into* The Divine, to arise and express again in another way on another day. The Divine is never not *within* us. It *is* us, manifesting as An Expression of Itself.

These can be useful metaphysical constructions, but frankly, I needed more. I've never been willing to swallow conjectures whole unless I felt they had at least some *possibility* of having a basis in fact, some at least partial grounding in reality as we now know it. So I sought to bring a little science into all this, just to balance the equation between metaphysics and physics.

What I found is that "reality as we know it" (or at least as *I* knew it) turns out to have very little to do with reality as it actually is.

Physicist and systems theorist Fritjof Capra tells us that "at the subatomic level, the solid material objects of classical physics dissolve into wave-like patterns of probabilities, and these patterns, ultimately, do not represent probabilities of things, but rather probabilities of interconnections.

"A careful analysis of the process of observation in atomic physics has shown that the subatomic particles have no meaning as isolated entities, but can only be understood as interconnections between the preparation of an experiment and the subsequent measurement.

"Quantum theory thus reveals a basic oneness of the universe.

"It shows that we cannot decompose the world into independently existing smallest units. As we penetrate into matter, nature does not show us any isolated 'basic building blocks' but rather appears as a complicated web of relations between the various parts of the whole." (—Capra. 2000 edition of *The Tao of Physics: An Exploration of the Parallels Between Modern Physics and Eastern Mysticism*, first published in 1975, p. 68)

That was enough for me. But I didn't stop there. Excited by what I had learned, I quietly undertook a layman's study of physics. Nothing academically deep, mind you. A book here, a book there over the months. But sufficient to convince me that even contemporary science has declared that everything is One Essence Manifesting Individually.

All of this brought up for me an interesting question. What is the connection between cosmology and theology? Are those who embrace the idea that they are an expression of The Divine rightly accused of heresy? Are they properly labeled apostates?

This was not unimportant to me, so I did a little theological research as well. I wanted to see what religious and spiritual sources had to say on the subject. I placed what I found in a small booklet titled *Recreating Yourself.*

I'm reprinting that research here, because I discovered—as

I had imagined must be true—that part of what humanity's Old Cultural Story was *telling us in the past* is what the New Cultural Story arising out of humanity's Daring Decision is *telling us now*.

Here's some of what I found . . .

Isaiah 41:23—*Shew the things that are to come hereafter, that we may know that ye are gods: yea, do good, or do evil, that we may be dismayed, and behold it together.*

Psalms 82:6—*I have said, "Gods ye are, And sons of the Most High—all of you."*

John 10:34—*Jesus answered them, Is it not written in your law, "I said, Ye are gods?"*

Sri Swami Krishnananda Saraswati Maharaj (April 25, 1922–November 23, 2001), a Hindu saint, said this: "*God exists; there is only one God; the essence of man is God.*"

According to Buddhism there ultimately is no such thing as a Self that is independent from the rest of the universe (the doctrine of *anatta*)—any more than there is a wave that is independent of the Ocean.

Also, if I understand certain Buddhist schools of thought correctly, humans return to the Earth in subsequent lifetimes in one of six forms, the last of which are called Devas . . . which is variously translated as *Gods* or *Deities*.

Meanwhile, the ancient Chinese discipline of Taoism speaks of embodiment and pragmatism, engaging practice to *actualize the Natural Order within themselves*. Taoists believe that man is a microcosm for the universe.

Hermeticism is a set of philosophical and religious beliefs or gnosis based primarily upon the Hellenistic Egyptian pseudepi-graphical writings attributed to Hermes Trismegistus. Hermeticism teaches that there is a transcendent God, The All, or one "Cause," in which we, and the entire universe, participate.

The concept was first laid out in *The Emerald Tablet of Hermes Trismegistus*, in the famous words: *"That which is Below corresponds to that which is Above, and that which is Above, corresponds to that which is Below, to accomplish the miracles of the One Thing."*

And in Sufism, an esoteric form of Islam, the teaching *There is no God but God* was long ago changed to *There is nothing but God.* Which would make us . . . well . . . *God.*

You might find it instructive and fascinating to get online and go to Wikipedia, the source to which I owe my appreciation for much of the above information.

But what of those who look to the words of Jesus for their counsel? Would they find the idea that God and we are One to be heretical? This is also not an unimportant question, so I looked more deeply into Jesus' words for guidance.

21

THE GUIDANCE

The words attributed to Jesus have become extremely important in the lives of billions the world over, so I wanted to find out if he was reported to have made any statements touching on this spiritually revolutionary idea of our all being one.

Using the Bible as my source, I found this statement:

"And for their sakes I sanctify myself that they also might be sanctified through the truth. Neither pray I for these alone, but for them also which shall believe on me through their word; That they all may be one; as thou, Father, art in me, and I in thee, that they also may be one in us: that the world may believe that thou hast sent me. And the glory which thou gavest me I have given them; that they may be one, even as we are one." (John 17:19–22)

I have concluded that Jesus lovingly understood our difficulty in believing that we are a part of God, part of God's very body. Yet Jesus did believe this of himself. It was therefore a simple matter (and a marvelous inspiration) for him to invite those who could not imagine *themselves* to be a part of God, to imagine themselves to be, in a very real sense, joined with *him*.

Jesus had already declared himself to be a part of God . . . and if we could simply believe that we were a part of the body of Christ, we would *by extension* necessarily be a part of God (whether we could find it in ourselves to declare that or not). And so it was that he said, "I am the vine, ye are the branches," describing for us our Oneness in him.

And here is what the author of 1 Corinthians 12–16, the Apostle Paul, gave us:

"For as the body is one, and hath many members, and all the members of that one body, being many, are one body: so also is Christ. For by one Spirit are we all baptized into one body, whether we be Jews or Gentiles, whether we be bound or free; and have been all made to drink into one Spirit. For the body is not one member, but many. If the foot shall say, Because l am not the hand, I am not of the body; is it therefore not of the body? And if the ear shall say, Because l am not the eye, l am not of the body; is it therefore not of the body?"

Jesus himself must have emphasized this point over and over, because every record of his teachings, and the commentaries upon them, in the Bible contain many references to this relationship.

String just a few of these separate references together and we have an extraordinary revelation:

I and my Father are one. (John 10:30)

And the glory which thou gavest me I have given them; that they may be one, even as we are one. (John 17:22)

I in them, and thou in me, that they may be made perfect in one. (John 17:23)

That the love wherewith thou hast loved me may be in them, and I in them. (John 17:26)

So we, being many, are one body in Christ; and every one members, one of another. (Romans 12:5)

Now he that planteth and he that watereth are one. (1 Cor. 3:8)

For we being many are one bread, and one body: for we are all partakers of that one bread. (1 Cor. 10:17)

But now are they many members, yet but one body. (1 Cor. 12:20)

You can't get much clearer than that.

22

THE IDEAS

We said early on in this exploration that ideas are important. We said it is ideas that create beliefs, beliefs that create behaviors, behaviors that create experience, and experience that creates reality. So let's look at some of the extraordinary ideas that could arise out of a decision to declare ourselves to be . . .

1. Spiritual Beings Manifesting Physically
2. One Essence Manifesting Individually

. . . and see if these might not be some of our most wonderful ideas ever. In my view they certainly could have a positive impact on our individual lives and, if embraced at a level of critical mass, on our world at large.

(Now you may think that reaching critical mass—getting to a level where one out of ten people become early adopters and add to what Everett Rogers, a professor of communication studies, called the "diffusion of innovation"—is unlikely to occur, or may even be impossible to achieve. Yet we notice that not one out of ten, but one of *four,* is now estimated to be using Facebook. This new behavior was adopted by one quarter of the human race in what, in cosmic terms, would be considered the blink of an eye. And so it may be not so impossible after all for the understanding and then the expression of our True Nature to reach critical mass.)

When enough people clearly see the accuracy of this understanding and the benefit of embracing and acting on it, a huge snowball will begin rolling downhill.

If human beings simply decided that we are both Spiritual Beings and One Being, our ideas about life could include these:

1. Life is an experience with a purpose greater than mere survival.

2. Everything that is occurring, both in our individual lives and in our collective experience, is serving that larger purpose perfectly.

3. Our experience of life is controllable to a much greater degree than we might have imagined.

4. Every event brings us benefit in some form.

5. It is not required for life to include suffering.

6. There is more going on here than meets the eye. The process of life is a process of our soul's evolution. This has nothing to do with worldly happiness—although worldly happiness is the inevitable product of the soul's evolutionary progress.

Our ideas about ourselves could include these:

1. We are in no way separate from each other, and we are all Individuations of Divinity, unique singularizations of the Essential Essence that is called, by some people, "God"—each of us an expression of The Divine, even as a wave arises from, and is an expression of, the Ocean.
2. We are all, because of this, wonderful in countless ways.
3. We are all capable of being everything we choose to be. (Not to be confused with everything we choose to *do* or to *have*. We are all capable of *being* Unconditionally Loving, Totally Conscious, Fully Aware, Truly Understanding, Profoundly Wise, Abundantly Clear, Endlessly Patient, Wonderfully Compassionate, Completely Accepting, Invariably Kind, Consistently Helpful, Remarkably Inspiring, and, in a word, Divine.)
4. We are all capable of living within the limitations and definitions of normal human experience without encountering prolonged unhappiness, confusion, hopelessness, or despair, by simply treating ourselves and each other differently.

Our ideas about God could include these:

1. God exists.
2. God is the Essential Essence in all of Creation, which could be called (to use a human analogy) the Stem Cell of the Universe—that is, the undifferentiated Pure and Eternal Energy that is the Source of all creation, all wis-

dom, of all understanding, all intelligence, and of all love, and that may shape and form Itself into countless and limitless physical or metaphysical manifestations, including every sentient being in the cosmos.

3. There is no separation between The Creator and The Created. Divinity is found in each of Divinity's Creations, as God is the All-in-All, the Alpha and the Omega, the Beginning and the End, the First and the Last, and is therefore absent from no one and nothing.

4. In God there is found love for each of us and everything in life, without condition, without limitation, and without a requirement to receive anything in return.

5. In God there is no need for anything, for in God there is lack of nothing and a yearning for nothing, since God is The Source and The Creator of everything and anything of which desire could even conceive.

6. In God there is no judgment, no condemnation, and no punishment for anything, given that we cannot in any way hurt, damage, injure, or anger that which God is.

7. In God we find the freedom and the power to create our own internal reality of the external events, occurrences, situations, and circumstances of our life.

8. In God we find the Essence that we call Love, which is the best single-word definition in every human language of Divinity, and in God we can feel that Essence embrace us and strengthen us whenever and however we seek that experience.

9. In God we find the Perfect Freedom to Create what it is our Will to Create, and in God we can experience a

personal relationship of Oneness and Unity, Singularity of Purpose, Desire, and Intention.

And finally, our ideas about what happens after death could include these:

1. We never stop existing, but will go on living forever and ever, in whatever form we may choose.
2. We will be reunited with everyone we have ever loved.
3. We will remain united with those who live after us in their present physical form. We will feel their love, and they will feel ours.
4. We will experience nothing but joy, freedom, total understanding, complete awareness, absolute serenity, and endless bliss, with the fullest knowing of anything and everything we wish to explore available to us at the speed of our thought.
5. We will be given the choice to return to the physical life we just left, and we may choose to, offering ourselves the opportunity to experience even more fully any aspect of that specific expression, or of the soul's overall and eternal agenda.
6. We will be given the opportunity to return to physical life at another place in what we call "time" and in another expression that we call an "incarnation," and we will do so, proceeding with the joyful and eternal purpose of Life Itself lifetime after lifetime, as we endlessly expand our experience and expression of Who We Really Are.

7. We may choose to move through succeeding lives in loving companionship with the one whom we have loved in our previous physical experience, as soul partners forever.

You may have difficulty accepting some of these ideas. They may be different from, and may actually violate, some of your own most deeply held beliefs. On the other hand, you may agree with all or most of them.

Either way, just for the intellectual excursion of it, just for the mental exercise, you're invited to take a moment to deeply explore all this, and then to ask yourself: What do you think would happen if humanity as a whole embraced these ideas? Do you think we'd be better off or worse off than we are now? What, if anything, do you think would change?

23

THE CHANGES

It may be intriguing to say that making one decision could change everything for the better, but every thinking person would want to know more about that. We've looked at some of the ideas, they would say, but not the *results* that could arise from making life's Daring Decision.

Honest skeptics would ask: What would be the on-the-ground *outcomes* if we reached critical mass in deciding that we are all Spiritual Beings/One Being? How would this look in "real life"?

Without stretching my imagination even a little, I can see these possibilities . . .

I believe that in our social constructions and conventions we would find ourselves leaving, and ultimately voluntarily dismantling and disavowing, exclusive groups, vested-interest organizations, government agencies, and all other societal structures and configurations that curb people's opportunities, segregate people's agendas, separate people's futures, limit people's rights, proportion people's benefits, restrict people's access, place opposition above cooperation in people's political undertakings, or generate adversarial, attacking, or injurious energies in *any* of people's activities.

In short, society in general would adhere to a new and enlightened motto: "Ours is not a better way, ours is merely another way." It would realize that there is more than one path to the mountaintop, and that the idea in any highly evolved civilization would not be to get to the summit first, but to get there together.

An advanced society would recognize that while it can be wonderful and effective to gather together under the umbrella of shared interests, to do so in a way that systematically eliminates people from participation based on race, religion, political persuasion, age, gender, or sexual orientation would be antithetical to the very reason for wishing to create a collective—which would presumably be to produce the most congenial fellowship, the greatest opportunity, and the highest good for all.

Thus, society would serve its highest purpose and its grandest function: to bring us, and to keep us, together as a species.

I believe that in our religions we would see the end of the seemingly endless competitions for human souls. Religions would stop insisting on portraying themselves as the One and Only Path to God. They would assist people in finding their own personal path, but they would not claim to *be* The Path. And they would cease using fear as their chief tool and their primary strategy.

They would stop teaching that unless people follow their doctrines, they are going to spend eternity in the everlasting fires of hell. They would be a source of comfort and guidance, of ever-present help, and of strength in times of need.

Thus, religion would serve its highest purpose and its grandest function: to open us to the possibility, the practicality, and the Presence of God—as well as the *presents* of God. It would be made clear that God's gifts are instantly available to everyone, without us having to yearningly hope, like children at a candy store window, for what we wish we could have, but what seems out of reach.

I believe that in our politics we would see the end of hidden agendas, of power plays, and of the demonization of those with alternate points of view. Political parties would stop claiming that their way is the only way. They would work together to find solutions to the most pressing problems, and to move society forward by seeking common ground.

They would seek to blend the most workable of their ideas with the most workable of the ideas of colleagues holding differing political positions. Thus, politics would serve its highest purpose and its grandest function: to create a process for cooperation and collaboration in improving the lives of citizens everywhere.

I believe that in our economics we would see the end of Bigger-Better-More as the international yardstick of Success. We would create a new Bottom Line, in which "maximum productivity" was redefined by a change in what we say we are seeking to *produce*. Our endless drive for profits-profits-*profits* would be replaced by a top-down commitment to create a world in which what we seek to produce is each person having an opportunity to live in dignity, with basic needs being met—a commitment driven by a sense of awe and wonder in the universe, and a reverence for all of life (not just our own).

Thus, economics would serve its highest purpose and its grandest function: to offer a way for members of a species to trade with, and to serve each other through, a process that allows the good of the whole to flow to all, with no one left behind to struggle and suffer and die while others roister and revel in more-than-could-possibly-be-needed luxuries.

These changes, and more, I see as our entire human species comes to realize that the two-part declaration I have called humanity's Most Important Decision neatly reduces to four words: *We Are All One.*

This is an amazing idea. Without wanting to sound sophomoric, it really could end war forever, redefine the way to resolve all disagreements, recreate the way we share all resources, and reinvent our very reason for living—for doing what we're doing and saying what we're saying, for having what we're having and seeking what we're seeking, for giving what we're giving and taking what we're taking, and for loving who and what we're loving.

It could thus change some of the choices we make in our own home, the words we use in our own dining room, the way we act in our own bed, the ideas that we hold in our own mind.

It could, to put it all in a simple phrase, *civilize civilization.* And that is what so many, many people are yearning for right now. Can we get back to being civilized? *Must* we be so polarized? Will we ever unlock our hearts again? What is the key?

24

THE KEY

As wonderful as all of the preceding may sound, there could be one final stumbling block in the way of some people fully embracing the idea that they are "one" with all others in the world.

Are we one with those who have done terrible things that we would never, ever, do? Are we to accept that we are unified with those who do the opposite of everything that we call good and loving and humane?

Even if the idea of our oneness reached critical mass and we created a society where horrific behavior would be almost entirely eliminated, what about the very few among us, the tiny minority, who might still act in such ways?

And what about those many more who would continue to do so under *today's* present social conditions, while our species is waiting to *reach* critical mass with the idea of its singularity?

This is another very fair question, for sure.

The answer is that it is possible for human beings to embrace their oneness with even those who might be labeled, by some, the worst of our species—and the key to making this decision easy may be summarized in one word. I'll give that to you in just a bit, but first, a "preamble."

An understanding of our Oneness does not call upon us to embrace the notion of "sameness." The words *inseparable* and *identical* are not synonymous. No one is suggesting that because we are all one, we are all the same.

The question then is: Can we accept that there is a part of the Unified Us that individuals within that Unified Us do not find attractive or acceptable? This question hits closer to home when it is asked in this way: Is there a part of *you* that you have ever found unattractive or unacceptable?

If your answer is no, then you might have a difficult time embracing the notion that other people who exhibit behaviors that are unacceptable to you are one with you, and that you are one with them.

Yet if you can remember a time when you have been or done something unattractive or unacceptable, then you may be able to understand how a person could do even horrible things (things you would never do), and you can begin to consider the understandings of Capra and many other physicists who tell us that everything *is* one thing—even though everything is not the same thing.

A spiritual teacher of mine once put this into marvelous perspective when she invited me to bring to mind those whom I judge to have acted in horrible ways. She challenged me to ponder how I think those I've judged might answer if they were asked what she called Life's Most Compassionate Question:

"What hurts you so much that you feel you have to hurt others in order to heal it?"

When I explored this question deeply, I found the key that opened me to seeing others in an entirely different way, because the question presumes that at the root of every person is inborn goodness, and that *this is the place where we are all one.*

This is the part of each other that we share. If others have stepped away from this part of themselves because of their pain, that doesn't mean that this part of themselves doesn't exist. It means that they have lost sight of it, but not that they have lost possession of it.

Here, then, is the key, in one word: Compassion.

Suddenly I found a way to not feel that I wanted to condemn others—not even those who have been called the worst among us. It happened the moment I gave thought to all they must have gone through in their lives to lead them to so completely abandon their True Nature and do what they did.

This does not justify their actions, nor does it mean that we condone them. But it does mean that we can understand them. Then we can rise above that urge to condemn, and even demonstrate mercy.

Too much to ask? More than might even be appropriate, given that some people are actually trying to kill us? Well, let's see.

On May 13, 1981, a man named Mehmet Ali Ağca shot Pope John Paul II repeatedly at close range as the Pope was traveling in an open car through St. Peter's Square in Vatican City. The assassination attempt left the Pope in great pain and very critical condition. The man was tackled, captured, tried, and sentenced to life in prison.

Though seriously injured and suffering acute blood loss from four bullet wounds—two in his lower intestine, one in his right arm, and one in his left hand—the Pope recovered, then asked all Catholics to pray for Ağca, saying that he had "sincerely forgiven" his assailant.

To accentuate the point, the Pontiff two years later visited Ağca in his cell. The two had a quiet conversation, and I wouldn't be surprised if the Pope posed some version of Life's Most Compassionate Question. Whatever was said, the pair became friends, shook hands warmly, and the Pope gave the man his Papal blessing.

He blessed the man who tried to kill him.

("But I say unto you, love your enemies, bless them that curse you, do good to them that hate you, and pray for them which despitefully use you, and persecute you . . .")

Wait. The story doesn't end there. In 2000 the Pontiff requested of the civil authorities that Ağca be pardoned. That request was granted.

Many people might have found it difficult, if not impossible, to do what Pope John Paul II did. That is because we are, as a species, so very young. As explained earlier, we are, on the scale of the universe, barely out of our infancy. Yet as our species matures spiritually, we will come to a profound understanding that will allow us to experience even more clearly our Oneness with everyone. And we will also see another enormous truth:

EVERY ACT IS AN ACT OF LOVE.

That was separated and boldfaced to highlight its importance on humanity's spiritual journey—a journey on which you are embarked more determinedly and consciously than ever in this very moment . . . lest you think that all you are reading here has come to you by accident.

You did not "chance" upon this book. You did not "happen" to see it. You knew, at some very deep level, that it offered, for all of humanity, what so many of us are looking for. A way out of this morass. A swath through the thicket. A stepping stone.

25

THE STEPPING STONE

It is true categorically and without exception, now and through-out all of human history, that there is not a single act, choice, or decision made by any human being that did not arise out of love.

In some cases, deeply distorted love, yes. In some very sad instances, mangled, twisted expressions of love, yes. But even the most heinous crime, the most horrible offense, was an expression of someone's love for something. When explored deeply, the accuracy of this statement is confirmed.

It is spiritual teachers who have told us: "Love is all there is." This is the foundation and the basis of the important insight that concluded the previous chapter, and is a stepping stone on the evolutionary path of our species.

If what so many spiritual teachers have said is true—if the Pure Energy and the Essential Essence of the universe that makes up the whole of the Universe is what is called, in human language, "love"—then all that exists must emerge from it, and must be an expression of it.

What, then, of fear? What of anger? What of hatred? What of evil? What of violence and killing? Surely, these can't be expressions of love.

But they are. If one didn't love something, one wouldn't fear anything. If one didn't love something, one wouldn't be angry about its opposite.

If a person (or a group) didn't love something desperately—some principle, some doctrine, some idea, some way of life, some person, or some physical possession—they couldn't even begin to think of using desperate measures as a means of getting it, keeping it, or protecting it.

If they didn't love something intensely, they could never be angry about either not having it, or having it taken from them.

Thieves act out of love. Terrorists act out of love. People who commit "crimes of passion" act out of love.

Again, to be clear, this doesn't condone their actions, but it does explain them. There is something—some object, experience, or outcome—that some love so much that they desperately want to have it, and because they know of, or think that there is, no other way to get it, they steal, they injure, they abuse, they kill.

The problem is not that human beings do not love, the problem is that too many human beings *act out* their love in ways that they, themselves, would never welcome. Put simply, not enough of us have learned how to do unto others as we would have done unto us.

You and I may not have done horrible, *horrible* things, but we each have done some things in our life that produced, on a much lower level, the same kind of result—injury to another—

and for the same reason: because we have expressed our love for someone or something in a way that hurt someone else.

Perhaps it was "being right" that we loved. Perhaps it was having our way. Perhaps it was power or wealth or a particular possession. Perhaps it was a particular experience, or being with a particular person. Whatever it was, it was our love of *this* that produced the hurting of *another.* Most of us have done this at least once in our life.

The only difference between us and others (other than the scale of things) is that we felt sure, in the moment that *we* made *our* choice, that our actions were understandable—or at least forgivable.

("All's fair in love and war" we were told, in the earliest known origin of that sentiment, found in poet John Lyly's novel *Euphues: The Anatomy of Wit*, way back in 1578. That's how long we've held *that* idea.)

The point: Love, as the Essential Essence of the Universe, is very powerful, and can produce highly impactful outcomes. It is important, then, to take great care in our expression of love. Yes, it may sound simplistic and jejune to say it, but it deserves being said nonetheless because, clearly, there are still not enough people who understand it. Just as nuclear energy can be used in a way that heats a city or destroys a city, the energy of love can be used in a way that heals or hurts, both people and the planet.

Yet behavior that destroys or injures would never be conceived of, much less acted out, if the people of Earth held as their most sacred belief that we are Spiritual Beings Physically Manifesting and One Essence Manifesting Individually.

And a person who fully understands this would respond to any deeply injuring act against another by asking themselves how the perpetrator would respond to a slightly altered version of Life's Most Compassionate Question: "What have you loved so much in your life that you feel you have to hurt others in order to experience it, protect it, or keep it?"

When we search for the answer to this question we see clearly, if sadly, that their acts were ultimately sponsored by love. Deeply distorted love, yes. Not condoned or approved of because of the explanation, no. But understood, and thus held in the mind of God (and in our mind if we choose God to be experienced as a part of us) in a different way.

26

THE DIFFERENT WAY

Can our species find a different way to be human? Can we create a new personal ethic, a new personal expression, a new personal experience? Can the average person—meaning you and me—actually stand as an exemplar?

Yes. All we have to do to solve the problems in our homes and in our world is gather the will to do so. And that occurs spontaneously in species that understand who they are and what they are.

There are such advanced beings in the Universe. They live in a different way, having long ago, in the earlier stages of their civilization's development (presumably, the stage at which we are now), made their Daring Decision. They chose to recognize that the Essential Essence (which some of us call God) was the singular ingredient of which they were comprised, and never to think of themselves in any other way.

The wonderful words of Maya Angelou come to mind here: "When we know better, we do better." Humanity is now getting to the place where we are beginning to know better. So each of us *can* choose—even if others do not—to know what "human nature" really is, and to express and experience it.

Then, even as we understand children whose immaturity and confusion leads to some of their actions, so, too, will we see that the same is true of adults who act in childish and hurtful ways. We'll be clear that *they don't know any better.*

We don't feel a deep need to "forgive" children when they behave childishly. The key I've talked about, the compassion I've described, arises naturally when we see their immaturity and confusion. We then find ourselves actually *comforting* them should they break the cherished family heirloom or play with matches and create mayhem.

This is an appropriate response with children, but is it with adults? Does it make sense to address the growing Alienation of fully grown humans in this way? Should we approach even those who have hurt us, or actually tried to kill us, and shake hands with them? I mean, what in the world was the Pope thinking?

Perhaps he was considering this: " Ye have heard that it hath been said, An eye for an eye, and a tooth for a tooth: But I say unto you, That ye resist not evil: but whosoever shall smite thee on thy right cheek, turn to him the other also. And if any man will sue thee at the law, and take away thy coat, let him have thy cloak also. And whosoever shall compel thee to go a mile, go with him twain."

And as for actually bestowing a *blessing* on the prisoner, perhaps these were the Pope's thoughts: "But I say unto you, Love your enemies, bless them that curse you, do good to them that hate you, and pray for them which despitefully use you, and persecute you; That ye may be the children of your Father which is in heaven: for he maketh his sun to rise on the evil and on the good, and sendeth rain on the just and on the unjust. For if ye love them which love you, what reward have ye? do not even the publicans the same? And if ye salute your brethren only, what do ye more than others? do not even the publicans so?"

(Comments? Questions, anyone? Is there some lack of clarity about what Jesus might have meant here?)

Jesus was not the only one to suggest that we love our enemies. The Buddha, centuries before him, advised his monks in the now famous Parable of the Saw that even if bandits were to savagely sever them limb by limb with a double-handled saw . . . "even then, whoever of you harbors ill will at heart would not be upholding my Teaching." He taught them to "remain full of concern and pity" for the attackers, with a mind of love, and not to give in to hatred.

And there have been other messengers as well—both ancient and contemporary, from widely varied cultural traditions—who have extended to us exactly the same invitation. So these are not new ideas. But what *may* be new in this present day is your determination to find a way to place those ideas into your life at the next level.

Yet the messages themselves are not enough. We need something else, something more, something new.

We need now to make a major choice. A Daring Decision. We need to *choose God* to be experienced as a part of *us*. This means consciously adopting, embracing, accepting, expressing, and experiencing that we are Spiritual Beings Physically Manifesting and One Essence Manifesting Individually.

But what is the *method* by which we can do that? We've

talked over and over about making that decision, so now the question is: *How does that work?* How do we express that choice in our daily life? How do we make that part of our moment-to-moment experience?

27

THE EXPERIENCE

Okay, what follows needn't be complicated or difficult. It can be challenging for sure, but "challenging" and "difficult" are not the same thing.

Anyone who has learned to ski and has done it well knows the difference. Anyone who has learned to make French *crêpes sucrées* and has done it well knows the difference. Anyone who has learned to speak a new language and has done it well knows the difference.

That which is continually "difficult" can be draining. That which is continually "challenging" can be invigorating. That's the difference.

Stepping into the living of your life as a Spiritual Being Physically Manifesting can be challenging, but it will be wonderfully invigorating once you feel the difference between moving through your life this way and the way most of us moved through our lives until we made this decision.

Stepping into the living of your life as One Essence Manifesting Individually can be even more challenging, because it places you on the fast track in your evolutionary process. But it can be even more than just invigorating. It can be revitalizing. Reviving. Restoring. Regenerating. Resuscitating. Rejuvenating. Reestablishing.

It *reestablishes* your true identity—an identity you may have set aside after you were told the Old Cultural Story about who you are and what human nature is and you accepted all of that as truth, even though it was not.

You now know that it is *not* "human nature" to think first of your own survival, that it is *not* "human nature" to refuse compassion, that it is *not* "human nature" to remain separate, and that it is *definitely* not "human nature" to feel Alienation.

You now know that being less than marvelously magnificent, less than wonderfully wise, less than completely clear, less than daringly Divine is *not* "human nature," *but just the opposite.*

Because we now know better, we can all now do better. We can now implement, actualize, *enact* our highest thoughts about Who and What We Are, turning them from concept to experience in our daily reality. This is the natural next step in our evolution.

Let me offer, from the For What It's Worth Dept., three tools that I've found to be wonderfully helpful as I seek not just to know, but to *express,* that I am a spiritual being living in a physical body, and that we are all individuations of a single essence. I don't use these tools as often as I would like (it's a matter of discipline—an area in which I am growing), but I'm better at it now than I ever was before, so I'm going to give myself that pat on the back, and encourage myself to keep on keeping on.

I invite you to do the same, whatever process and methods you might use.

Tool #1 offers me a way to embrace the first aspect of my True Nature—that I am not just a physical entity, but a spiritual being. Because I choose to express myself as a spiritual being, I have begun asking myself a simple but powerful question several times a day. You could call it my Beingness Question.

I ask this question internally if I am thinking of watching a television program or going to a movie. I ask it of myself if I am invited to a gathering of some kind. I pose the question if I'm browsing through my books to find something to read, or browsing through my fridge to find something to eat.

I try to remember to ask it of myself before I make *any* decision that's going to create an experience of myself in a particular way on this particular day. I also ask it if I'm encountering a particularly difficult or frustrating moment. Perhaps a plan of mine isn't going well, or maybe I'm having a tiff with a loved one.

Here's the question:

What does this have to do with the agenda of my soul?

Almost instantly, whenever I ask myself that question, I get my answer. Either what I'm about to do or say resonates with my soul's agenda or it does not. And I know it immediately. And I see the choice that is before me as an opportunity for growth— for expanding into the full experience of my True Nature.

If I'm experiencing one of life's difficult moments, the answer to my Beingness Question allows me to see such a moment in a new way as well—not as an obstacle, but as an opportunity for growth.

Now I know that may sound just shy of unbelievably trite, but growth can actually become a welcome and exciting prospect when I understand what I am doing here. That is, why I came to Earth.

I *came* here for growth. I *came* here for expansion. And I came here as part of an eternal journey that does not begin and end with my birth and death in this "lifetime."

For me to transform every moment of choice in my life from seeming meaningless to being meaningful, and every moment of difficulty in my life from seeming disagreeable to being agreeable, I must be clear that the agenda of my soul is to recreate myself anew, in every Golden Moment of Now, in the next grandest version of the greatest vision ever I held about Who I Am.

In other words, creation. *Continual* creation. Continual Creation of the *Self.* (Which, we ultimately realize, is not self-creation in the truest sense at all, but, in the truest sense, *Self Realization.* We are not actually creating who we are, but coming to know and experience who we are at the next level.)

Given an awareness of this agenda (which I believe to be the agenda we all share, called "evolution"), I have placed at my fingertips a way to experience myself as a spiritual being. I simply contextualize my daily encounters and choices within a new framework—the framework formed by my spiritual identity and my spiritual purpose, both of which are eternal.

Tool #2 is the making of a firm commitment to strive to experience that aspect of myself that I know to be One Essence Manifesting Individually. I have found it easier than I ever thought it could be, by asking myself a different question at very specific points in my day.

These are moments when I feel myself moved by emotion,

either positively or negatively, as I observe, experience, or notice someone or something that appears to be separate from me. It could be a sunset. Or a sudden and scary windstorm. It could be another person being wonderfully caring of me and very loving. Or it could be an instance such as I described earlier, when a person is being aggressive, and maybe even a little confronting.

It could be someone whose behavior I am observing at a distance or across the room. Whatever it is I am observing that I notice is bringing up an emotion in me, I ask myself a second question that I may, if I wish, combine with the first. You could call this my Oneness Question.

Here's the question:

Is there any part of what I am now seeing "over there" that I have seen "over here"—in myself?

If I see a beautiful and glorious sunset, is there a part of me that is beautiful and glorious, of which it arouses an awareness in me? If I hear of a person who has been unbelievably courageous (perhaps someone who has run out into traffic and saved someone's life), is there a part of me that is unbelievably courageous, of which it arouses an awareness in me?

If I see or hear of a person who is being or has been domineering or self-serving, or even unkind and hurtful, is there a part of me that is or has been domineering or self-serving, or even unkind and hurtful, that it arouses an awareness of in me?

Whether I'm observing something or someone magnificent, or something or someone less than magnificent, I allow myself to see if I can find some version of that in myself. This, more than any other device or tool I've heard of or used, has helped me to feel—to actually *experience*—the part of me that's being shown to me.

If and when I see myself outside of myself, it is then that I realize that there *is* no such place. I see that "outside of myself" does not exist; that there is nothing "outside of myself" that I do not find "inside of myself" at some level, to some degree, in some proportion. And it is then that I can experience and show true compassion for the person in whom I see The Same Thing Larger. Or, perhaps, The Same Thing Smaller.

Ultimately, I stop measuring, I stop comparing, to see who's Larger or Smaller in the ways that I am. I stop looking to see who's "better" or "worse," who's "more" or "less." I see Only Me outside of me, "acting out" a part of me that's inside of me—that I have *experienced* there.

If it's a part of me that pleases me, and it brings me joy to think of myself in that way, I determine to demonstrate more of that as my life goes on. If it is a part of me with which I am not pleased, and it saddens me to think of myself in that way, I commit to demonstrating less and less of that as my life goes on.

So if you want the Experience of Oneness, and are not content to just dabble in the Concept, and if you want the Experience of your Spirituality, and are not content to just dabble in the Concept, try these two questions some time. See if they work for you as they have for me.

Tool #3 invites me to pay continuing attention to how this idea of choosing God to be experienced as a part of me can be recognized by me as having already been part of my life. I have come to see that I, *and you,* have *already done this.* We've simply called it something else.

Some years ago I wrote a book titled *Communion with God*. It was written entirely from God's point of view, and not long after it reached bookstores, reporters began calling me for interviews, many of them leading with the same question: Where do you get off speaking in the First Person Voice of God? Isn't that more than a little presumptuous?

It's another one of those fair questions. While I am not the first person to have produced such a book (far from it, in fact), inquiring minds still want to know: How can I—or for that matter, anyone—dare to place words in God's mouth in this way?

The first thing I answer when asked this question is that I am not placing words in God's mouth. God is placing words in mine. Furthermore, God is doing the same thing with *all of us*. I am not the only person on the planet speaking God's words.

All of us are in communion with God all of the time. All of us, including you, have spoken in the First Person Voice of God.

If you have ever spoken of love to any other person, you have spoken in the First Person Voice of God.

If you have ever spoken of compassion to a person in need of compassion, you have spoken in the First Person Voice of God.

If you have ever spoken of forgiveness to a person who seeks forgiveness (or even to one who does not—perhaps especially to one who does not), you have spoken in the First Person Voice of God.

If you have ever argued for fairness, called for justice, pleaded for peace, recommended mercy, or proposed a win-win solution to anyone, you have spoken in the First Person Voice of God.

If you have ever consoled or comforted, encouraged or motivated, uplifted or congratulated, you have spoken in the First Person Voice of God.

If you have ever renewed another's faith (especially in themselves), restored another's hope, revived another's dream, confirmed another's greatness, you have spoken in the First Person Voice of God.

If you have ever respected another's truth, resolved another's doubt, removed another's fear, recalled another's goodness, recited another's attributes, reduced another's apprehension, relieved another's mind, or remained another's friend, you have spoken in the First Person Voice of God.

It is not difficult to speak in the First Person Voice of God. It is more difficult not to. You have to step away from, you have to *abandon,* your True Nature.

When you let God place words in your mouth, you always speak the truth, you always speak with sensitivity and awareness, you always speak of how to resolve, not who to blame.

You always speak your mind, but you always speak from the heart, and you always speak with the wisdom and gentleness of your soul. You speak your truth, but soothe your words with peace.

Every moment is a moment of Communion with God . . . and we can experience it as that if we consciously reject from Separation Theology and choose God to be part of us.

So as you speak the words you speak today—whatever those words might be—ask yourself, "Is this what I want the world to hear from God right now?"

Imagine what your life would be like if you decided that every word you uttered was the Word of God.

Does that feel like too much responsibility? Is that more than you wish to carry on your shoulders?

Well, too bad. Because every word you utter IS the Word of God . . . unless the essence of you and the essence of God *are* completely separated and are *not* "one"—in which case everything you've read in this book is out the window.

Yet I can understand how it could feel like a lot of responsibility. But what if you did not see this as a burden, but rather, as an opportunity? What if you saw it as your chance to simply step into your grandest thought about what Divinity is, in any and every moment that you choose to do so?

If you saw it as that—as an "invitation," not a "requirement"—your whole life could suddenly become a great adventure. Each day you would awaken with massive excitement, asking yourself, "What does God want to say to the world today, through me?"

That's an intriguing question, isn't it? I mean, supposing you were to ask yourself that every morning: "What does God want to say to the world today, through me?"

So I invite us all today to look a little more closely at what we are putting out into the world. And to see if, perhaps, we may want to make a little adjustment. You know, here or there . . . once in a while . . . now and then . . . to bring Our Pronouncements closer to God's Announcements.

Does that feel to you like a worthy experiment for you to undertake this week?

I think you'll find that all three of these tools can be very impactful in your life, really helping you to not just *conceptualize* yourself as a Spiritual Being Physically Manifesting and One Essence Manifesting Individually, but to *experience* yourself as that.

Actually, there is a whole *list* of ways you can do this. I've left that for our finale.

28

THE FINALE

We're all doing our best here, but let's not kid each other. This is not an easy road that we're traveling. The journey from birth to death is no picnic. It *can* be more joyful . . . more fulfilling, and more wonderful . . . if we know Who and What We Are. If we know that we are, in *fact*, Spiritual Beings/One Being.

Sadly, no one told us this in school. No one taught us this at our place of worship. No one discussed this at the dinner table in our home. No one supplied us with this information when we were young, to prepare us to enter into adult life. This is the info they never gave us.

And so, we've had no accurate idea (if we had any idea at all) of how we got here or where we're going after we leave here—much less how we can make it all work *while* we're here.

Now, here in this little book, I've offered what I hope you have found to be some compelling information about what's going on here on the planet and why, and some useful suggestions on ways that all of us can express and experience our True Nature in spite of what's going on—and thus begin to change what's going on.

Let me present here, as a finale to this exploration, an actual *list* of such ways.

This list was given to us in the text of the book *Conversations with God,* Book 4: *Awaken the Species.* It describes sixteen differences in the behavior of an awakened species when compared to the behavior of humans living in an unawakened state. I am reprinting the list here because I believe that humanity benefits enormously when helpful information is repeated as often as possible.

Let us see, then, what it would be like to experience our True Nature at the highest level.

1. An awakened species sees the Unity of All Life and lives into it. Humans in an unawakened state often deny it or ignore it.

2. An awakened species tells the truth, always. Humans in an unawakened state too often lie, to themselves as well as others.

3. An awakened species says one thing and will do what they say. Humans in an unawakened state often say one thing and do another.

4. An awakened species, having seen and acknowledged what is so, will always do what works. Humans in an unawakened state often do the opposite.

5. An awakened species does not embrace a principle in its civilization that correlates with the concepts that humans refer to as "justice" and "punishment."

6. An awakened species does not embrace a principle in its

civilization that correlates with the concept that humans refer to as "insufficiency."

7. An awakened species does not embrace a principle in its civilization that correlates with the concept that humans refer to as "ownership."

8. An awakened species shares everything with everyone all the time. Humans in an unawakened state often do not, only sharing with others in limited circumstances.

9. An awakened species creates a balance between technology and cosmology; between machines and nature. Humans in an unawakened state often do not.

10. An awakened species would never under any circumstances terminate the current physical expression of another sentient being unless asked directly by that other being to do so. Humans in an unawakened state often kill other humans without that other human requesting them to.

11. An awakened species would never do anything that could potentially damage or harm the physical environment that supports the members of the species when they are physicalized. Humans in an unawakened state often do so.

12. An awakened species never poisons itself. Humans in an unawakened state often do so.

13. An awakened species never competes. Humans in an unawakened state are often in competition with each other.

14. An awakened species is clear that it needs nothing. Humans in an unawakened state often create a need-based experience.

15. An awakened species experiences and expresses unconditional love for everyone. Humans in an unawakened state often cannot imagine even a Deity who does this, much less do they do it themselves.

16. An awakened species has harnessed the power of metaphysics. Humans in an unawakened state often largely ignore it.

When I've read this list in lectures or retreats, people invariably asked me to speak about it in greater detail. All of the items are explored extensively in the text of this book, of course, but here's a brief exploration of the two that I am most often asked about . . . #4 and #8.

About #4, regarding doing what works:

If your objective is to live a life of peace, joy, and love, *violence does not work.* This has *already been demonstrated.* We do the opposite anyway.

If your objective is to live a life of good health and great longevity, consuming dead flesh daily, smoking known carcinogens, and drinking gallons of nerve-deadening, brain-frying liquids regularly *does not work.* This has *already been demonstrated.* We do the opposite anyway.

If your objective is to raise offspring free of violence and rage, placing them directly in front of movies, television programs, and even *games* with vivid depictions of violence and rage during their most impressionable years *does not work*. This has *already been demonstrated*. We do the opposite anyway.

If your objective is to care for Earth and wisely husband her resources, acting as if those resources are limitless *does not work*. This has *already been demonstrated*. We do the opposite anyway.

If your objective is to discover and cultivate a relationship with a loving Deity so that religion can make a difference in the affairs of humans, then teaching of a god of righteousness, punishment, and terrible retribution *does not work*. This has *already been demonstrated*. We do the opposite anyway.

About #8, regarding sharing everything with everyone all the time:

Sharing does not mean giving away everything you have to everyone you know or meet. It means freely sharing of your time, talents, gifts, resources, and abundance with those who have need of them—but not in a way that depletes all that you have, leaving *you* with nothing more to share. It means giving a *share* of what you have, not giving *all* of what you have. That's why it's called *sharing* and not *alling*. And it means sharing not only with those who are closest to you, but wherever you see a need and may be able to offer some help.

I believe that all of the behaviors of a fully awakened species will spontaneously arise in humans when we choose the Essential Essence that we call Divinity to be experienced as a part of us, and as that of which all beings and all aspects of life are comprised.

I believe that our personal decisions and choices, actions and priorities will change dramatically when we inwardly confirm that the presence of the spirit of God within is a normal aspect of our daily life, and then decide to recognize Divinity at last for what it has always been: our True Nature.

You, yourself, are the evidence of this. I want to make these points once again, so that you never forget them. You have not been told this often enough. Indeed, some religions have actually told all of us that we are sinners; that we were *born* in sin—"original sin" it has been called—and that we are far from Divine.

Yet the fact that God lives within you is revealed in every gift of self you have ever offered, in any form, to any other person whose life you have touched with the miracle of love. For if love expressed *through* you is not the evidence of God *in* you, then nothing is.

Divinity shines through you every time someone is brightened by your smile, every time someone is restored by your recognition of their gifts, every time someone is renewed by your honoring of their virtues and your reminder of their worthiness—and surely every time someone is remembered with love in your heart.

In these moments you couldn't deny the presence of Divinity within you if you tried. You feel it, you know it, and whatever your personal philosophy or theology allows you to call it, you deeply understand that it is your True Nature.

You have been, in many, many moments of your life, goodness and mercy and compassion and understanding. You have been forgiveness and patience, strength and courage, a helper in someone's time of need, a comforter in someone's time of sorrow, a healer in someone's time of injury, a teacher in someone's time of confusion. You have been in many moments the deepest wisdom and the highest truth; the greatest companion and the grandest love.

Your soul knows Who You Are, and now your mind is choosing to accept what your soul has known and been telling you all along. You are a Spiritual Being Manifesting Physically and One Essence Manifesting Individually.

This is an Essence shared by everyone and everything in existence.

Is there any remaining doubt as to what this Essence is?

No.

So be it.

I mean that literally. So *be it*.

I want to conclude my sharing with you in this book with these thoughts from the American poet Em Claire, whom I am blessed to call my wife.

*I don't know if my god is
the same as your god:*

*Is it made of Love?
Does it want for you
what* you *want for you?
Does it come to you
with hands opened,
asking nothing,
but ready for anything?*

Does it whisper to you
of Light and of Stillness,
and point you toward
any of the paths
that will take you there?

Does it remind you
of your Seeing?
Does it remind you
of your Knowing?
Does it remind you
of the Gentlest Lover
ever you've dreamed,
caressing a weariness
from your heart?

Is it ever late?

Is it ever gone?
Is it made of Love?

AFTERWORD

Readers of my previous writings may recognize some of the points made in this book from online postings, social media entries, or passages in an earlier book from me.

If so, I thank you for indulging me in my determination to continue to place before people everywhere, even at the risk of repetition, a life altering, world changing message (for which I do not take credit, but which was given to me in a series of dialogues which I published under the title *Conversations with God*).

I believe the problem of increasing Alienation among the people of this planet to be not a small dilemma on this day, and I am clear about what can heal the hurt and the divisions caused by the increasingly hardened stances being taken by individuals and organizations, political parties and special interest groups, governments and even religions, as we move deeper into the 21st century.

I appreciate the opportunity to share these ideas with you here, and I hope that you agree with them. Agree or not, however, you are welcome to share your views with me. I am always interested in any questions about, or comments relating to, these concepts—especially as they relate to your experience of the state of the world today.

If you feel it will serve you to do so, I invite you to stay connected with the energy you've found here by joining me and others from across the globe at www.CWGConnect.com. Let's see if we can, together, move toward critical mass in the number of us choosing now to embark on The Essential Path.

Let's take a look at the dictionary to better understand the description of this path.

> ESSENTIAL: Fundamental or central to the nature of something or someone. A thing that is absolutely necessary.

I believe the path leading to the embracing of our True Nature is fundamental and central to the fullest expression of "human nature." Indeed, I see it as an *absolutely necessary* next step in the evolution of humanity.

I know that it's taken longer than Victor Hugo would have hoped, but I nevertheless echo his belief in unstoppable humanistic progress. It was Mr. Hugo who also said: "All the forces in the world are not so powerful as an idea whose time has come." His calculation of when that time would arrive was not accurate, but the thrust of his observation most certainly was.

I believe that today, because of the power that humanity has acquired to rapidly spread an idea globally, we have arrived at that time. And we can now choose to unravel all that we have strung together over the centuries on this planet which has produced the world of stress and struggle that so many know it to be today. We can make the daring decision to declare ourselves to be Spiritual Beings Manifesting Physically and One Essence Manifesting Individually.

As evidenced here, this idea is in alignment with the Biblical and spiritual messages from ages past. I'll leave you now with a parting thought from a more contemporary source, my sweet friend and a wonderfully wise and fully integrated person . . . Eckhart Tolle:

"In the stillness of your presence, you can feel your own formless and timeless reality as the unmanifested life that animates your physical form. You can then feel the same life deep within every other human and every other creature. You look beyond the veil of form and separation. This is the realization of oneness. This is love."

ABOUT THE AUTHOR

Neale Donald Walsch is the author of more than thirty-five books combining modern-day psychology and practical spirituality. His titles have sold in the millions, and have been translated into over 30 languages. He may be reached on his online platform CWGConnect, which arose out of his worldwide work surrounding the Conversations with God series of books.